Andrew Lang, Gordon Browne

My own fairy book

Andrew Lang, Gordon Browne
My own fairy book
ISBN/EAN: 9783743345348

Manufactured in Europe, USA, Canada, Australia, Japa

Cover: Foto ©ninafisch / pixelio.de

Manufactured and distributed by brebook publishing software (www.brebook.com)

Andrew Lang, Gordon Browne

My own fairy book

My Own Fairy Book,

namely certain Chronicles of Pantouflia, as notably the Adventures of Prigio, Prince of that country, and of his son, Ricardo, with an Excerpt from the Annals of Scotland, as touching Ker of Fairnilee, his sojourn with the Queen of Faery; the whole written by Andrew Lang and adorned by Gordon Browne, T. Scott, and E. A. Lemann.

Bristol:
Arrowsmith.

1895.

New York:
Longmans, Green & Co.

MY OWN FAIRY BOOK.

CONTENTS.

To Children ix

Prince Prigio.

Chap.		Page
I.	HOW THE FAIRIES WERE NOT INVITED TO COURT	5
II.	PRINCE PRIGIO AND HIS FAMILY . . .	10
III.	ABOUT THE FIREDRAKE	14
IV.	HOW PRINCE PRIGIO WAS DESERTED BY EVERYBODY	23
V.	WHAT PRINCE PRIGIO FOUND IN THE GARRET .	28
VI.	WHAT HAPPENED TO PRINCE PRIGIO IN TOWN .	30
VII.	THE PRINCE FALLS IN LOVE	38
VIII.	THE PRINCE IS PUZZLED	43
IX.	THE PRINCE AND THE FIREDRAKE . . .	48
X.	THE PRINCE AND THE REMORA	51
XI.	THE BATTLE	54
XII.	A TERRIBLE MISFORTUNE	60
XIII.	SURPRISES	67
XIV.	THE KING EXPLAINS	70
XV.	THE KING'S CHEQUE	77
XVI.	A MELANCHOLY CHAPTER	83
XVII.	THE BLACK CAT AND THE BRETHREN . .	89
XVIII.	THE VERY LAST	99

Prince Ricardo.

Chap.		Page
	INTRODUCTORY	107
I.	THE TROUBLES OF KING PRIGIO	109
II.	PRINCESS JAQUELINE DRINKS THE MOON	120
III.	THE ADVENTURE OF THE SHOPKEEPERS	132
IV.	TWO LECTURES	142
V.	PRINCE RICARDO CROSSES THE PATH OF HISTORY	154
VI.	RICARDO'S REPENTANCE	171
VII.	PRINCE RICARDO AND AN OLD ENEMY	180
VIII.	THE GIANT WHO DOES NOT KNOW WHEN HE HAS HAD ENOUGH	195
IX.	PRIGIO HAS AN IDEA	207
X.	THE END	220

The Gold of Fairnilee.

I.	THE OLD HOUSE	237
II.	HOW RANDAL'S FATHER CAME HOME	239
III.	HOW JEAN WAS BROUGHT TO FAIRNILEE	245
IV.	RANDAL AND JEAN	251
V.	THE GOOD FOLK	259
VI.	THE WISHING WELL	263
VII.	WHERE IS RANDAL?	270
VIII.	THE ILL YEARS	277
IX.	THE WHITE ROSES	284
X.	OUT OF FAIRYLAND	289
XI.	THE FAIRY BOTTLE	296
XII.	AT THE CATRAIL	300
XIII.	THE GOLD OF FAIRNILEE	304

TO CHILDREN.

THE *Author* of this book is also the *Editor* of the *Blue, Red, Green, and Yellow Fairy Books.* He has always felt rather an impostor, because so many children seem to think that he made up these books out of his own head. Now he only picked up a great many old fairy tales, told in French, German, Greek, Chinese, Red Indian, Russian, and other languages, and had them translated and printed, with pictures. He is glad that children like them, but he must confess that they should be grateful to old forgotten people, long ago, who first invented these tales, and who knew more about fairies than we can hope to do.

My Own Fairy Book, which you now have

in your hands, was made up altogether out of his own head by the Author, of course with the help of the Historical Papers in the kingdom of Pantouflia. About that ancient kingdom very little is known. The natives speak German; but the Royal Family, as usual, was of foreign origin. Just as England has had Norman, Scottish, and, at present, a line of German monarchs, so the kings of Pantouflia are descended from an old Greek family, the Hypnotidæ, who came to Pantouflia during the Crusades. They wanted, they explained, not to be troubled with the Crusades, which they thought very injudicious and tiresome. The Crest of the regal house is a Dormouse, dormant, proper, on a field vert, and the Motto, when translated out of the original Greek, means, *Anything for a Quiet Life.*

It may surprise the young reader that princes like Prigio and Ricardo, whose feet were ever in the stirrup, and whose lances were always in rest, should have descended from the family of the Hypnotidæ, who were remarkably lazy and peaceful. But these heroes doubtless inherited the spirit of their great ancestress, whose story is necessary to be known. On leaving his native realm during the Crusades, in search of some secure asylum, the founder of the Pantouflian monarchy landed in the island of Cyprus, where, during the noon-tide heat, he lay down to sleep in a cave. Now in this cave dwelt a dragon of enormous size and unamiable character. What was the horror of the exiled prince when he was aroused from slumber by the fiery breath of the dragon, and felt its scaly coils about him!

"Oh, hang your practical jokes!" exclaimed the prince, imagining that some of his courtiers were playing a prank on him.

"Do you call *this* a joke?" asked the

dragon, twisting its forked tail into a line with his royal highness's eye.

"Do take that thing away," said the prince, "and let a man have his nap peacefully."

"KISS ME!." cried the dragon, which had already devoured many gallant knights for declining to kiss it.

"Give you a kiss," murmured the prince; "oh, certainly, if that's all! *Anything for a quiet life.*"

So saying, he kissed the dragon, which instantly became a most beautiful princess; for she had lain enchanted as a dragon, by a wicked magician, till somebody should be bold enough to kiss her.

"My love! my hero! my lord! how long I have waited for thee; and now I am eternally thine own!"

So murmured, in the most affectionate accents, the Lady Dragonissa, as she was now called.

Though wedded to a bachelor life, the prince was much too well-bred to make any remonstrance.

The Lady Dragonissa, a female of extraordinary spirit, energy, and ambition, took command of him and of his followers, conducted them up the Danube, seized a principality whose lord had gone crusading, set her husband on the throne, and became in course of time the mother of a little prince, who, again, was great, great, great, great-grandfather of our Prince Prigio.

From this adventurous Lady Dragonissa, Prince Prigio derived his character for gallantry. But her husband, it is said, was often heard to remark, by a slight change of his family motto:

"*Anything for a Quiet Wife!*"

You now know as much as the Author does of the early history of Pantouflia.

As to the story called *The Gold of Fairnilee*,

such adventures were extremely common in Scotland long ago, as may be read in many of the works of Sir Walter Scott and of the learned in general. Indeed, Fairnilee is the very place where the fairy queen appointed to meet her lover, Thomas the Rhymer.

With these explanations, the Author leaves to the judgment of young readers his *Own Fairy Book.*

PRINCE PRIGIO

PRINCE PRIGIO

IS

Dedicated

TO

ALMA

THYRA

EDITH

ROSALIND

NORNA

CECILY

AND VIOLET

PREFACE.

IN compiling the following History from the Archives of Pantouflia, the Editor has incurred several obligations to the Learned. The Return of Benson (chapter xii.) is the fruit of the research of the late Mr. ALLEN QUATERMAIN, while the final *wish* of Prince Prigio was suggested by the invention or erudition of a Lady.

A study of the *Firedrake* in South Africa— where he is called the *Nanaboulélé*, a difficult word—has been published in French (translated from the Basuto language) by M. PAUL SÉBILLOT, in the *Revue des Traditione Populaires*. For the *Remora*, the Editor is indebted to the *Voyage à la Lune* of M. CYRANO DE BERGÉRAC.

CHAPTER I.

How the Fairies were not Invited to Court.

ONCE upon a time there reigned in Pantouflia a king and a queen. With almost everything else to make them happy, they wanted one thing: they had no children. This vexed the king even more than the queen, who was very clever and learned, and who had hated dolls when she was a child. However, she too, in spite of all the books she read and all the pictures she painted, would have been glad enough to be the mother of a little prince. The king was anxious to consult the fairies, but the queen would not hear of such a thing. She did not believe in fairies: she said that they had never existed; and that she maintained, though *The History of the Royal Family* was full of chapters about nothing else.

Well, at long and at last they had a little boy, who was generally regarded as the finest baby that had ever been seen. Even her majesty herself remarked that, though she could never believe all the courtiers told her, yet he certainly was a fine child—a very fine child.

Now, the time drew near for the christening party, and the king and queen were sitting at breakfast in their summer parlour talking over it. It was a splendid room, hung with portraits of the royal ancestors. There was Cinderella, the grandmother of the reigning monarch, with her little foot in her glass slipper thrust out before her. There was the Marquis de Carabas, who, as everyone knows, was raised to the throne as prince consort after his marriage with the daughter of the king of the period. On the arm of the throne was seated his celebrated cat, wearing boots. There, too, was a portrait of a beautiful lady, sound asleep: this was Madame La Belle au Bois-dormant, also an ancestress of the royal family. Many other pictures of celebrated persons were hanging on the walls.

"You have asked all the right people, my dear?" said the king.

"Everyone who should be asked," answered the queen.

"People are so touchy on these occasions," said his majesty. "You have not forgotten any of our aunts?"

"No; the old cats!" replied the queen; for the king's aunts were old-fashioned, and did not approve of her, and she knew it.

"They are very kind old ladies in their way," said the king; "and were nice to me when I was a boy."

Then he waited a little, and remarked:

"The fairies, of course, you have invited? It has always been usual, in our family, on an occasion like this; and I think we have neglected them a little of late."

"How *can* you be so *absurd?*" cried the queen. "How often must I tell you that there are *no* fairies? And even if there were—but, no matter; pray let us drop the subject."

"They are very old friends of our family, my dear, that's all," said the king timidly. "Often and often they have been godmothers to us. One, in particular, was most kind and most serviceable to Cinderella I., my own grandmother."

"Your grandmother!" interrupted her majesty. "Fiddle-de-dee! If anyone puts such nonsense into the head of my little Prigio——"

But here the baby was brought in by the nurse, and the queen almost devoured it with kisses. And so the fairies were not invited! It was an extraordinary thing, but none of the nobles could come to the christening party when they learned that the fairies had not been asked. Some were abroad; several were ill; a few were in prison among the Saracens; others were captives in the dens of ogres. The end of it was that the king and queen had to sit down alone, one at each end of a very long table, arrayed with plates and glasses for a hundred guests — for a hundred guests who never came!

"Any soup, my dear?" shouted the king, through a speaking-trumpet; when, suddenly, the air was filled with a sound like the rustling of the wings of birds.

Flitter, flitter, flutter, went the noise; and when the queen looked up, lo and behold! on every seat was a lovely fairy, dressed in green, each with a *most interesting-looking parcel* in her hand. Don't you like opening parcels? The king did, and he was most friendly and polite to the fairies. But the queen, though she saw them distinctly, took no notice of them. You see, she did not believe in fairies, nor in her own eyes, when she saw them. So she talked across the fairies to the king, just as if they had not been there; but the king behaved as politely as if they were *real*—which, of course, they were.

When dinner was over, and when the nurse

had brought in the baby, all the fairies gave him the most magnificent presents. One offered a purse which could never be empty; and one a pair of seven-leagued boots; and another a cap of darkness, that nobody might see the prince when he put it on; and another a wishing-cap; and another a carpet, on which, when he sat, he was carried wherever he wished to find himself. Another made him beautiful for ever; and another, brave; and another, lucky: but the last fairy of all, a cross old thing, crept up and said, "My child, you shall be *too* clever!"

This fairy's gift would have pleased the queen, if she had believed in it, more than anything else, because she was so clever herself. But she took no notice at all; and the fairies went each to her own country, and none of them stayed there at the palace, where nobody believed in them, except the king, a little. But the queen tossed all their nice boots and caps, carpets, purses, swords, and all, away into a dark lumber-room; for, of course, she thought that they were *all nonsense*, and merely old rubbish out of books, or pantomime "properties."

CHAPTER II.

Prince Prigio and his Family.

WELL, the little prince grew up. I think I've told you that his name was Prigio—did I not? Well, that *was* his name. You cannot think how clever he was. He argued with his nurse as soon as he could speak, which was very soon. He argued that he did not like to be washed, because the soap got into his eyes. How-ever, when he was told all about the *pores of the skin,* and how they could not be healthy if he was not washed, he at once ceased to resist, for he was very reasonable. He argued with his father that he did not see why there should be kings who were rich, while beggars were

poor; and why the king—who was a little greedy—should have poached eggs and plumcake at afternoon tea, while many other persons went without dinner. The king was so surprised and hurt at these remarks that he boxed the prince's ears, saying, "I'll teach you to be too clever, my lad." Then he remembered the awful curse of the oldest fairy, and was sorry for the rudeness of the queen. And when the prince, after having his ears boxed, said that "force was no argument," the king went away in a rage.

Indeed, I cannot tell you how the prince was hated by all! He would go down into the kitchen, and show the cook how to make soup. He would visit the poor people's cottage, and teach them how to make the beds, and how to make plum pudding out of turnip-tops, and venison cutlets out of rusty bacon. He showed the fencing-master how to fence, and the professional cricketer how to bowl, and instructed the rat-catcher in breeding terriers. He set sums to the Chancellor of the Exchequer, and assured the Astronomer Royal that the sun does not go round the earth—which, for my part, I believe it does. The young ladies of the court disliked dancing with him, in spite of his good looks, because he was always asking, "Have you read this?" and "Have you read that?"—and when they said they hadn't, he sneered; and when they said they *had*, he found them out.

He found out all his tutors and masters in the same horrid way; correcting the accent of his French teacher, and trying to get his German tutor not to eat peas with his knife. He also endeavoured to teach the queen-dowager, his grandmother, an art with which she had long been perfectly familiar! In fact, he knew everything better than anybody else; and the

worst of it was that he *did:* and he never was in the wrong, and he always said, "Didn't I tell you so?" And, what was more, he *had!*

As time went on, Prince Prigio had two younger brothers, whom everybody liked. They were not a bit clever, but jolly. Prince Alphonso, the third son, was round, fat, good-humoured, and as brave as a lion. Prince Enrico, the second, was tall, thin, and a little sad, but *never* too clever. Both were in love with two of their own cousins (with the approval of their dear parents); and all the world said, "What nice, unaffected princes they are!" But Prigio nearly got the country into several wars by being too clever for the foreign ambassadors. Now, as Pantouflia was a rich, lazy country, which hated fighting, this was very unpleasant, and did not make people love Prince Prigio any better.

CHAPTER III.

About the Firedrake.

OF all the people who did not like Prigio, his own dear papa, King Grognio, disliked him most. For the king knew he was not clever himself. When he was in the counting-house, counting out his money, and when he happened to say, "Sixteen shillings and fourteen and twopence are three pounds, fifteen," it made him wild to hear Prigio whisper, "One pound, ten and twopence,"—which, of course, it *is*. And the king was afraid that Prigio would conspire, and get made king himself—which was the last thing Prigio really wanted. He much preferred to idle about, and know everything without seeming to take any trouble.

Well, the king thought and thought. How was he to get Prigio out of the way, and make Enrico or Alphonso his successor? He read in books about it; and all the books showed that, if a king sent his three sons to do anything, it was always the youngest who did it, and got the crown. And he wished he had the chance. Well, it arrived at last.

There was a very hot summer! It began to be hot in March. All the rivers were dried up. The grass did not grow. The corn did not grow. The thermometers exploded with heat. The barometers stood at SET FAIR. The people were much distressed, and came and broke the palace windows—as they usually do when things go wrong in Pantouflia.

The king consulted the learned men about the Court, who told him that probably a

FIREDRAKE

was in the neighbourhood.

Now, the Firedrake is a beast, or bird, about the bigness of an elephant. Its body is made of iron, and it is always red-hot. A more terrible and cruel beast cannot be imagined; for, if you go near it, you are at once broiled by the Firedrake.

But the king was not ill-pleased: "for," thought he, "of course my three sons must go after the brute, the eldest first; and, as usual, it will kill the first two, and be beaten by the youngest. It is a little hard on Enrico, poor boy; but *anything* to get rid of that Prigio!"

Then the king went to Prigio, and said that his country was in danger, and that he was determined to leave the crown to whichever of them would bring him the horns (for it has horns) and tail of the Firedrake.

"It is an awkward brute to tackle," the king said, "but you are the oldest, my lad; go where glory waits you! Put on your armour, and be off with you!"

This the king said, hoping that either the Firedrake would roast Prince Prigio alive (which he could easily do, as I have said; for he is all over as hot as a red-hot poker), or that, if the prince succeeded, at least his country would be freed from the monster.

But the prince, who was lying on the sofa doing sums in compound division, for fun, said in the politest way:

"Thanks to the education your majesty has given me, I have learned that the Firedrake, like the siren, the fairy, and so forth, is a fabu-

"PUT ON YOUR ARMOUR AND BE OFF WITH YOU!"

lous animal which does not exist. But even granting, for the sake of argument, that there is a Firedrake, your majesty is well aware that there is no kind of use in sending *me*. It is always the eldest son who goes out first, and comes to grief on these occasions, and it is always the third son that succeeds. Send Alphonso" (this was the youngest brother), "and *he* will do the trick at once. At least, if he fails, it will be most unusual, and Enrico can try his luck."

Then he went back to his arithmetic and his slate, and the king had to send for Prince Alphonso and Prince Enrico. They both came in very warm; for they had been whipping tops, and the day was unusually hot.

"Look here," said the king, "just you two younger ones look at Prigio! You see how hot it is, and how coolly he takes it, and the country suffering; and all on account of a Firedrake, you know, which has apparently built his nest not far off. Well, I have asked that lout of a brother of yours to kill it, and he says——"

"That he does not believe in Firedrakes," interrupted Prigio. "The weather's warm enough without going out hunting!"

"Not believe in Firedrakes!" cried Alphonso. "I wonder what you *do* believe in! Just let me get at the creature!" for he was as brave as a lion. "Hi! Page, my chain-armour, helmet, lance, and buckler! *A Molinda! A Molinda!*" which was his *war-cry*.

The page ran to get the armour; but it was *so uncommonly hot* that he dropped it, and put his fingers in his mouth, crying!

"You had better put on flannels, Alphonso, for this kind of work," said Prigio. "And if I were you, I'd take a light garden-engine, full of water, to squirt at the enemy."

"Happy thought!" said Alphonso. "I will!" And off he went, kissed his dear Molinda, bade her keep a lot of dances for him (there was to be a dance when he had killed the Firedrake), and then he rushed to the field!

But he never came back any more!

Everyone wept bitterly—everyone but Prince Prigio; for he thought it was a practical joke, and said that Alphonso had taken the opportunity to start off on his travels and see the world.

"There is some dreadful mistake, sir," said Prigio to the king. "You know as well as I do that the youngest son has always succeeded, up to now. But I entertain great hopes of Enrico!"

And he grinned; for he fancied it was all *nonsense*, and that there were no Firedrakes.

Enrico was present when Prigio was consoling the king in this unfeeling way.

"Enrico, my boy," said his majesty, "the task awaits you, and the honour. When *you* come back with the horns and tail of the Firedrake, you shall be crown prince; and Prigio shall be made an usher at the Grammar School —it is all he is fit for."

Enrico was not quite so confident as Alphonso had been. He insisted on making his will; and he wrote a poem about the pleasures and advantages of dying young. This is part of it:

> *The violet is a blossom sweet,*
>   *That droops before the day is done—*
> *Slain by thine overpowering heat,*
>   *O Sun!*
>
> *And I, like that sweet purple flower,*
>   *May roast, or boil, or broil, or bake,*
> *If burned by thy terrific power,*
>   *Firedrake!*

This poem comforted Enrico more or less, and he showed it to Prigio. But the prince only laughed, and said that the second line of the last verse was not very good; for violets do not "roast, or boil, or broil, or bake."

Enrico tried to improve it, but could not. So he read it to his cousin, Lady Kathleena, just as it was; and she cried over it (though I don't think she understood it); and Enrico cried a little, too.

However, next day he started, with a spear, a patent refrigerator, and a lot of the bottles people throw at fires to put them out.

But *he* never came back again!

After shedding torrents of tears, the king summoned Prince Prigio to his presence.

"Dastard!" he said. "Poltroon! *Your* turn, which should have come first, has arrived at last. *You* must fetch me the horns and the tail of the Firedrake. Probably you will be grilled, thank goodness; but who will give me back Enrico and Alphonso?"

"Indeed, your majesty," said Prigio, "you must permit me to correct your policy. Your only reason for dispatching your sons in pursuit of this dangerous but I believe *fabulous* animal, was to ascertain which of us would most worthily succeed to your throne, at the date—long may it be deferred!—of your lamented decease. Now, there can be no further question about the matter. I, unworthy as I am, represent the sole hope of the royal family. Therefore to send me after the Firedrake were* both dangerous and unnecessary. Dangerous, because, if he treats me as you say he did my brothers— my unhappy brothers,—the throne of Pantouflia will want an heir. But, if I do come back alive—why, I cannot be more the true heir than

* Subjunctive mood! He was a great grammarian!

I am at present; now *can* I ? Ask the Lord Chief Justice, if you don't believe *me*."

These arguments were so clearly and undeniably correct that the king, unable to answer them, withdrew into a solitary place where he could express himself with freedom, and give rein to his passions.

CHAPTER IV.

How Prince Prigio was deserted by Everybody.

MEANWHILE, Prince Prigio had to suffer many unpleasant things. Though he was the crown prince (and though his arguments were unanswerable), everybody shunned him for a coward. The queen, who did not believe in Firedrakes, alone took his side. He was not only avoided by all, but he had most disagreeable scenes with his own cousins, Lady Molinda and Lady Kathleena. In the garden Lady Molinda met him walking alone, and did not bow to him.

"Dear Molly," said the prince, who liked her, "how have I been so unfortunate as to offend you?"

"My name, sir, is Lady Molinda," she said, very proudly; "and you have sent your own brother to his grave!"

"Oh, excuse me," said the prince, "I am certain he has merely gone off on his travels. He'll come back when he's tired: there *are* no Firedrakes; a French writer says they are 'purement fabuleux,' purely fabulous, you know."

"MY NAME SIR, IS LADY MOLINDA, SHE SAID."

"Prince Alphonso has gone on his travels, and will come back when he is tired! And was he then — tired — of *me?*" cried poor Molinda, bursting into tears, and forgetting her dignity.

"Oh! I beg your pardon, I never noticed; I'm sure I am very sorry," cried the prince, who, never having been in love himself, never thought of other people. And he tried to take Molinda's hand, but she snatched it from him and ran away through the garden to the palace, leaving Prince Prigio to feel foolish, for once, and ashamed.

As for Lady Kathleena, she swept past him like a queen, without a word. So the prince, for all his cleverness, was not happy.

After several days had gone by, the king returned from the solitary place where he had been speaking his mind. He now felt calmer and better; and so at last he came back to the palace. But on seeing Prince Prigio, who was lolling in a hammock, translating Egyptian hieroglyphs into French poetry for his mother, the king broke out afresh, and made use of the most cruel and impolite expressions.

At last, he gave orders that all the Court should pack up and move to a distant city; and that Prince Prigio should be left alone in the palace by himself. For he was quite unendurable, the king said, and he could not trust his own temper when he thought of him. And he grew so fierce, that even the queen was afraid of him now.

The poor queen cried a good deal; Prigio being her favourite son, on account of his acknowledged ability and talent. But the rest of the courtiers were delighted at leaving Prince Prigio behind. For his part, he, very good-naturedly, showed them the best and shortest road to Falkenstein, the city where they were going; and easily proved that neither the chief secretary for geography, nor the general of the army, knew anything about the matter—which, indeed, they did not.

The ungrateful courtiers left Prigio with hoots and yells, for they disliked him so much that they forgot he would be king one day. He therefore reminded them of this little fact in future history, which made them feel uncomfortable enough, and then lay down in his hammock and went to sleep.

When he wakened, the air was cold and the day was beginning to grow dark. Prince Prigio thought he would go down and dine at a tavern in the town, for no servants had been left with him. But what was his annoyance when he found that his boots, his sword, his cap, his cloak—all his clothes, in fact, except those he wore,—had been taken away by the courtiers, merely to spite him! His wardrobe had been ransacked, and everything that had not been carried off had been cut up, burned, and destroyed. Never was such a spectacle of wicked mischief. It was as if hay had been made of everything he possessed. What was worse, he had not a penny in his pocket to buy new things; and his father had stopped his allowance of fifty thousand pounds a month.

Can you imagine anything more cruel and *unjust* than this conduct? for it was not the prince's fault that he was so clever. The cruel fairy had made him so. But, even if the prince had been born clever (as may have happened to you), was he to be blamed for that? The other people were just as much in fault for being born so stupid; but the world, my dear children, can never be induced to remember this. If you are clever, you will find it best not to let people know it—if you want them to like you.

Well, here was the prince in a pretty plight. Not a pound in his pocket, not a pair of boots to wear, not even a cap to cover his head from the rain; nothing but cold meat to eat, and never a servant to answer the bell.

CHAPTER V.

What Prince Prigio found in the Garret.

THE prince walked from room to room of the palace; but, unless he wrapped himself up in a curtain, there was nothing for him to wear when he went out in the rain. At last he climbed up a turret-stair in the very oldest part of the castle, where he had never been before; and at the very top was a little round room, a kind of garret. The prince pushed in the door with some difficulty—not that it was locked, but the handle was rusty, and the wood had swollen with the damp. The room was very dark; only the last grey light of the rainy evening came through a slit of a window, one of those narrow windows that they used to fire arrows out of in old times.

But in the dusk the prince saw a heap of all sorts of things lying on the floor and on the table. There were two caps; he put one on—an old, grey, ugly cap it was, made of felt. There was a pair of boots; and he kicked off his slippers, and got into *them*. They were a good deal worn, but fitted as if they had been made for him. On the table was a purse with just three gold coins—old ones, too—in it; and this, as you may fancy, the prince was very well pleased to put in his pocket. A sword, with a sword-belt, he buckled about his waist; and the rest of the articles, a regular collection of odds and ends, he left just where they were lying. Then he ran downstairs, and walked out of the hall door.

CHAPTER VI.

What Happened to Prince Prigio in Town.

BY this time the prince was very hungry. The town was just three miles off; but he had such a royal appetite, that he did not like to waste it on bad cookery, and the people of the royal town were bad cooks.

"I wish I were in 'The Bear,' at Gluckstein," said he to himself; for he remembered that there was a very good cook there. But, then, the town was twenty-one leagues away—sixty-three long miles!

No sooner had the prince said this, and taken just three steps, than he found himself at the door of the "Bear Inn" at Gluckstein!

"This is the most extraordinary dream," said he to himself; for he was far too clever, of course, to believe in seven-league boots. Yet he had a pair on at that very·moment, and it was they which had carried him in three strides from the palace to Gluckstein!

The truth is, that the prince, in looking about the palace for clothes, had found his way into that very old lumber-room where the magical gifts of the fairies had been thrown by his clever mother, who did not believe in them. But this, of course, the prince did not know.

Now you should be told that seven-league boots only take those prodigious steps when you say you *want* to go a long distance. Otherwise they would be very inconvenient—when you only want to cross the room, for example. Perhaps this has not been explained to you by your governess?

Well, the prince walked into "The Bear," and it seemed odd to him that nobody took any notice of him. And yet his face was as well known as that of any man in Pantouflia; for everybody had seen it, at least in pictures. He was so puzzled by not being attended to as usual, that *he quite forgot to take off his cap.*

He sat down at a table, however, and shouted *"Kellner!"* at which all the waiters jumped, and looked round in every direction, but nobody came to him.

At first he thought they were too busy, but presently another explanation occurred to him

"The king," said he to himself, "has threatened to execute anybody who speaks to me, or helps me in any way. Well, I don't mean to starve in the midst of plenty, anyhow; here goes!"

The prince rose, and went to the table in the midst of the room, where a huge roast turkey had just been placed. He helped himself to half the breast, some sausages, chestnut stuffing, bread sauce, potatoes, and a bottle of red wine—Burgundy. He then went back to a table in a corner, where he dined very well, nobody taking any notice of him. When he had finished, he sat watching the other people dining, and smoking his cigarette. As he was sitting thus, a very tall man, an officer in the uniform of the Guards, came in, and, walking straight to the prince's table, said: "Kellner, clean this table, and bring in the bill of fare."

With these words, the officer sat down suddenly in the prince's lap, as if he did not see him at all. He was a heavy man, and the prince, enraged at the insult, pushed him away and jumped to his feet. As he did so, *his cap dropped off*. The officer fell on his knees at once, crying:

"Pardon, my prince, pardon! I never saw you!"

This was more than the prince could be expected to believe.

"Nonsense! Count Frederick von Matterhorn," he said; "you must be intoxicated. Sir! you have insulted your prince and your superior officer. Consider yourself under arrest! You shall be sent to a prison to-morrow."

On this, the poor officer appealed piteously to everybody in the tavern. They all declared that they had not seen the prince, nor ever had an idea that he was doing them the honour of being in the neighbourhood of their town.

More and more offended, and convinced that there was a conspiracy to annoy and insult him, the prince shouted for the landlord, called for his bill, threw down his three pieces of gold without asking for change, and went into the street.

"It is a disgraceful conspiracy," he said. "The king shall answer for this! I shall write to the newspapers at once!"

He was not put in a better temper by the way in which people hustled him in the street. They ran against him exactly as if they did not see him, and then staggered back in the greatest surprise, looking in every direction for the person they had jostled. In one of these encounters, the prince pushed so hard against a poor old beggar woman that she fell down. As he was usually most kind and polite, he pulled off his cap to beg her pardon, when, behold, the beggar woman gave one dreadful scream, and fainted! A crowd was collecting, and the prince, forgetting that he had thrown down all his money in the tavern, pulled out his purse. Then he remembered what he had done, and expected to find it empty; but, lo, there were three pieces of gold in it! Overcome with surprise, he thrust the money into the woman's hand, and put on his cap again. In a moment the crowd, which had been staring at him, rushed away in every direction, with cries of terror, declaring that there was a magician in the town, and a fellow who could appear and disappear at pleasure!

By this time, you or I, or anyone who was not so extremely clever as Prince Prigio, would have understood what was the matter. He had put on, without knowing it, not only the seven-league boots, but the cap of darkness, and had taken Fortunatus's purse, which could never be empty, however often you took all the money out. All those and many other delightful wares the fairies had given him at his christening, and the prince had found them in the dark garret. But the prince was so extremely wise, and learned, and scientific, that he did not believe in fairies, nor in fairy gifts.

"It is indigestion," he said to himself: "those sausages were not of the best; and that Burgundy was extremely strong. Things are not as they appear."

Here, as he was arguing with himself, he was nearly run over by a splendid carriage and six, the driver of which never took the slightest

notice of him. Annoyed at this, the prince leaped up behind, threw down the two footmen, who made no resistance, and so was carried to the door of a magnificent palace. He was determined to challenge the gentleman who was in the carriage; but, noticing that he had a very beautiful young lady with him, whom he had never seen before, he followed them into the house, not wishing to alarm the girl, and meaning to speak to the gentleman when he found him alone.

A great ball was going on; but, as usual, nobody took any notice of the prince. He walked among the guests, being careful not to jostle them, and listening to their conversation.

It was all about himself! Everyone had heard of his disgrace, and almost everyone cried "Serve him right!" They said that the airs he gave himself were quite unendurable—that nothing was more rude than to be always in the right—that cleverness might be carried far too far—that it was better even to be born stupid ("Like the rest of you," thought the prince); and, in fact, nobody had a good word for him.

Yes, one had! It was the pretty lady of the carriage. I never could tell you how pretty she was. She was tall, with cheeks like white roses blushing: she had dark hair, and very large dark-grey eyes, and her face was the kindest in the world! The prince first thought how nice and good she looked, even before he thought how pretty she looked. *She* stood up for Prince Prigio when her partner would speak ill of him. She had never seen the prince, for she was but newly come to Pantouflia; but she declared that it was his *misfortune*, not his fault, to be so clever. "And, then, think how hard they made him work at school! Besides," said this kind young lady, " I hear he is extremely handsome, and very brave; and he has a good heart, for he was kind, I have heard, to a poor boy, and did all his examination papers for him, so that the boy passed first in *everything*. And now he is Minister for Education, though he can't do a line of Greek prose!"

The prince blushed at this, for he knew his conduct had not been honourable. But he at once fell over head and ears in love with the young lady, a thing he had never done in his life before, because—he said—" women were so stupid!" You see he was so clever!

Now, at this very moment—when the prince, all of a sudden, was as deep in love as if he had been the stupidest officer in the room—an extraordinary thing happened! Something seemed to give a whirr! in his brain, and in one instant *he knew all about it!* He believed in fairies and fairy gifts, and understood that his cap was the cap of darkness, and his shoes the seven-league boots, and his purse the purse of Fortunatus! He had read about those things in historical books: but now he believed in them.

4 *

CHAPTER VII.

The Prince Falls in Love.

HE understood all this, and burst out laughing, which nearly frightened an old lady near him out of her wits. Ah! how he wished he was only in evening dress, that he might dance with the charming young lady. But there he was, dressed just as if he were going out to hunt, if anyone could have seen him. So, even if he took off his cap of darkness, and became visible, he was no figure for a ball. Once he would not have cared, but now he cared very much indeed.

But the prince was not clever for nothing. He thought for a moment, then went out of the room, and, in three steps of the seven-league boots, was at his empty, dark, cold palace again. He struck a light with a flint and steel, lit a torch, and ran upstairs to the garret. The flaring light of the torch fell on the pile of "rubbish," as the queen would have called it, which he turned over with eager hands. Was there—yes, there *was* another cap! There it lay, a handsome green one with a red feather.

The prince pulled off the cap of darkness, put on the other, and said:

"*I wish I were dressed in my best suit of white and gold, with the royal Pantouflia diamonds!*"

In one moment there he was in white and gold, the greatest and most magnificent dandy in the whole world, and the handsomest man!

"How about my boots, I wonder," said the prince; for his seven-league boots were stout riding-boots, not good to dance in, whereas *now* he was in elegant shoes of silk and gold.

He threw down the wishing cap, put on the other—the cap of darkness—and made three strides in the direction of Gluckstein. But he was only three steps nearer it than he had been, and the seven-league boots were standing beside him on the floor!

"No," said the prince; "no man can be in two different pairs of boots at one and the same time! That's mathematics!"

He then hunted about in the lumber-room again till he found a small, shabby, old Persian carpet, the size of a hearthrug. He went to his own room, took a portmanteau in his hand, sat down on the carpet, and said:

"I wish I were in Gluckstein."

In a moment there he found himself; for this was that famous carpet which Prince Hussein bought long ago, in the market at

Bisnagar, and which the fairies had brought, with the other presents, to the christening of Prince Prigio.

When he arrived at the house where the ball was going on, he put the magical carpet in the portmanteau, and left it in the cloak-room, receiving a numbered ticket in exchange. Then he marched in all his glory (and, of course, without the cap of darkness) into the room where they were dancing. Everybody made place for him, bowing down to the ground, and the loyal band struck up *The Prince's March:*

> *Heaven bless our Prince Prigio!*
> *What is there he doesn't know?*
> *Greek, Swiss, German (High and Low),*
> *And the names of the mountains in Mexico,*
> *Heaven bless the prince!*

He used to be very fond of this march, and the words—some people even said he had made them himself. But now, somehow, he didn't much like it. He went straight to the Duke of Stumpfelbahn, the Hereditary Master of the Ceremonies, and asked to be introduced to the beautiful young lady. She was the daughter of the new English Ambassador, and her name was Lady Rosalind. But she nearly fainted when she heard who it was that wished to dance with her, for she was not at all particularly clever; and the prince had such a bad character for snubbing girls, and asking them difficult questions. However, it was impossible to refuse, and so she danced with the prince, and he danced very well. Then they sat out in the conservatory, among the flowers, where nobody came near them; and then they danced again, and then the Prince took her down to supper. And all the time he never once said, "Have you read *this?*" or "Have you read *that?*" or, "What! you never heard of Alexander the Great?" or Julius Cæsar, or Michael Angelo, or whoever it might be—horrid, difficult questions he used to ask. That was the way he *used* to go on: but now he only talked to the young lady about *herself;* and she quite left off being shy or frightened, and asked him all about his own country, and about the Firedrake shooting, and said how fond she was of hunting herself. And the prince said:

"Oh, if *you* wish it, you shall have the horns and tail of a Firedrake to hang up in your hall, to-morrow evening!"

Then she asked if it was not very dangerous work, Firedrake hunting; and he said it was nothing, when you knew the trick of it: and he asked her if she would but give him a rose out of her bouquet; and, in short, he made himself so agreeable and *unaffected*, that she thought him very nice indeed.

For, even a clever person can be nice when he likes—above all, when he is not thinking about himself. And now the prince was thinking of nothing in the world but the daughter of the English Ambassador, and how to please her. He got introduced to her father too, and quite won his heart; and, at last, he was invited to dine next day at the Embassy.

In Pantouflia, it is the custom that a ball must not end while one of the royal family goes on dancing. *This* ball lasted till the light came in, and the birds were singing out of doors, and all the mothers present were sound asleep. Then nothing would satisfy the prince, but that they all should go home singing through the streets; in fact, there never had been so merry a dance in all Pantouflia.

The prince had made a point of dancing with almost every girl there: and he had suddenly become the most beloved of the royal family. But everything must end at last; and the prince, putting on the cap of darkness and sitting on the famous carpet, flew back to his lonely castle.

CHAPTER VIII.

The Prince is Puzzled.

PRINCE PRIGIO did not go to bed. It was bright daylight, and he had promised to bring the horns and tail of a Firedrake as a present to a pretty lady. He had said it was easy to do this; but now, as he sat and thought over it, he did not feel so victorious.

"First," he said, "where is the Firedrake?"

He reflected for a little, and then ran upstairs to the garret.

"It *should* be here!" he cried, tossing the fairies' gifts about; "and, by George, here it is!"

Indeed, he had found the spyglass of carved ivory which Prince Ali, in the *Arabian Nights*, bought in the bazaar in Schiraz. Now, this glass was made so that, by looking through it, you could see anybody or anything you wished, however far away. Prigio's first idea was to look at his lady. "But she does not expect to be looked at," he thought; "and I *won't!*" On the other hand, he determined to look at the Firedrake; for, of course, he had no delicacy about spying on *him*, the brute.

The prince clapped the glass to his eye, stared out of window, and there, sure enough, he saw the Firedrake. He was floating about in a sea of molten lava, on the top of a volcano. There he was, swimming and diving for pleasure, tossing up the flaming waves, and blowing fountains of fire out of his nostrils, like a whale spouting!

The prince did not like the looks of him.

"With all my cap of darkness, and my shoes of swiftness, and my sword of sharpness, I never could get near that beast," he said; "and if I *did* stalk him, I could not hurt him. Poor little Alphonso! poor Enrico! what plucky fellows they were! I fancied that there was no such thing as a Firedrake: he's not in the

Natural History books; and I thought the boys were only making fun, and would be back soon, safe and sound. How horrid being too clever makes one! And now, what *am* I to do?"

What was he to do, indeed? And what would you have done? Bring the horns and tail he must, or perish in the adventure. Otherwise, how could he meet his lady?—why, she would think him a mere braggart.

The prince sat down, and thought and thought; and the day went on, and it was now high noon.

At last he jumped up and rushed into the library, a room where nobody ever went except himself and the queen. There he turned the books upside down, in his haste, till he found an old one, by a French gentleman, Monsieur Cyrano de Bergerac. It was an account of a voyage to the moon, in which there is a great deal of information about matters not generally known; for few travellers have been to the moon. In that book, Prince Prigio fancied he would find something he half remembered, and that would be of use to him. And he *did!* So you see that cleverness, and minding your book, have some advantages, after all. For here the prince learned that there is a very rare beast called a Remora, which is at least as cold as the Firedrake is hot!

"Now," thought he, "*if I can only make these two fight*, why the Remora may kill the Fire-

THE REMORA   ✳

drake, or take the heat out of him, at least, so that I may have a chance."

Then he seized the ivory glass, clapped it to his eye, and looked for the Remora. Just the tip of his nose, as white as snow and as smooth as ice, was sticking out of a chink in a frozen mountain, not far from the burning mountain of the Firedrake.

"Hooray!" said the prince softly to himself; and he jumped like mad into the winged shoes of swiftness, stuck on the cap of darkness, girdled himself with the sword of sharpness, and put a good slice of bread, with some cold tongue, in a wallet, which he slung on his back. Never you fight, if you can help it, except with plenty of food to keep you going and in good heart. Then off he flew, and soon he reached the volcano of the Firedrake.

CHAPTER IX.

The Prince and the Firedrake.

IT was dreadfully hot, even high up in the air, where the prince hung invisible. Great burning stones were tossed up by the volcano, and nearly hit him several times. Moreover, the steam and smoke, and the flames which the Firedrake spouted like foam from his nostrils, would have daunted even the bravest man. The sides of the hill, too, were covered with the blackened ashes of his victims, whom he had roasted when they came out to kill him. The garden-engine of poor little Alphonso was lying in the valley, all broken and useless. But the Firedrake, as happy as a wild duck on a lonely lock, was rolling and diving in the liquid flame, all red-hot and full of frolic.

"Hi!" shouted the prince.

The Firedrake rose to the surface, his horns as red as a red crescent-moon, only bigger, and lashing the fire with his hoofs and his blazing tail.

"Who's there?" he said in a hoarse, angry voice. "Just let me get at you!"

"It's me," answered the prince. It was the first time he had forgotten his grammar, but he was terribly excited.

"What do you want?" grunted the beast. "I wish I could see you"; and, horrible to relate, he rose on a pair of wide, flaming wings, and came right at the prince, guided by the sound of his voice.

Now, the prince had never heard that Firedrakes could fly; indeed, he had never believed in them at all, till the night before. For a moment he was numb with terror; then he flew down like a stone to the very bottom of the hill and shouted:

"Hi!"

"Well," grunted the Firedrake, "what's the matter? Why can't you give a civil answer to a civil question?"

"Will you go back to your hole and swear, on your honour as a Firedrake, to listen quietly?"

"On my sacred word of honour," said the beast, casually scorching an eagle that flew by into ashes. The cinders fell, jingling and crackling, round the prince in a little shower.

Then the Firedrake dived back, with an awful splash of flame, and the mountain roared round him.

The prince now flew high above him, and cried:

"A message from the Remora. He says you are afraid to fight him."

"Don't know him," grunted the Firedrake.

"He sends you his glove," said Prince Prigio, "as a challenge to mortal combat, till death do you part."

Then he dropped his own glove into the fiery lake.

"Does he?" yelled the Firedrake. "Just let me get at him!" and he scrambled out, all red-hot as he was.

"I'll go and tell him you're coming," said the prince; and with two strides he was over the frozen mountain of the Remora.

CHAPTER X.

The Prince and the Remora.

IF he had been too warm before, the prince was too cold now. The hill of the Remora was one solid mass of frozen steel, and the cold rushed out of it like the breath of some icy beast, which indeed it *was*. All around were things like marble statues of men in armour: they were the dead bodies of the knights, horses and all, who had gone out of old to fight the Remora, and who had been frosted up by him. The prince felt his blood stand still, and he grew faint; but he took heart, for there was no time to waste. Yet he could nowhere see the Remora.

"Hi!" shouted the prince.

Then, from a narrow chink at the bottom of the smooth, black hill,—a chink no deeper than that under a door, but a mile wide,—stole out a hideous head!

It was as flat as the head of a skate-fish, it

was deathly pale, and two chill-blue eyes, dead-coloured like stones, looked out of it.

Then there came a whisper, like the breath of the bitter east wind on a wintry day:

"Where are you, and how can I come to you?"

"Here I am!" said the prince from the top of the hill.

Then the flat, white head set itself against the edge of the chink from which it had peeped, and slowly, like the movement of a sheet of ice, it slipped upwards and curled upwards, and up, and up! There seemed no end to it at all; and it moved horribly, without feet, holding on by its own frost to the slippery side of the frozen hill. Now all the lower part of the black hill was covered with the horrid white thing coiled about it in smooth, flat shiny coils; and still the head was higher than the rest; and still the icy cold came nearer and nearer, like Death.

The prince almost fainted: everything seemed to swim; and in one moment more he would have fallen stiff on the mountain-top, and the white head would have crawled over him, and the cold coils would have slipped over him and turned him to stone. And still the thing slipped up, from the chink under the mountain.

But the prince made a great effort; he moved, and in two steps he was far away, down in the valley where it was not so very cold.

"Hi!" he shouted, as soon as his tongue could move within his chattering teeth.

There came a clear, hissing answer, like frozen words dropping round him:

"Wait till I come down. What do you want?"

Then the white folds began to slide, like melting ice, from the black hill.

Prince Prigio felt the air getting warmer behind him, and colder in front of him.

He looked round, and there were the trees beginning to blacken in the heat, and the grass looking like a sea of fire along the plains; for the Firedrake was coming!

The prince just took time to shout, "The Firedrake is going to pay you a visit!" and then he soared to the top of a neighbouring hill, and looked on at what followed.

CHAPTER XI.

The Battle.

IT was an awful sight to behold! When the Remora heard the name of the Firedrake, his hated enemy, he slipped with wonderful speed from the cleft of the mountain into the valley. On and on and on he poured over rock and tree, as if a frozen river could slide downhill; on and on, till there were miles of him stretching along the valley—miles of the smooth-ribbed, icy creature, crawling and slipping forwards. The green trees dropped their leaves as he advanced; the birds fell down dead from the sky, slain by his frosty breath! But, fast as the Remora stole forward, the Firedrake came quicker yet, flying and clashing his fiery wings. At last they were within striking distance; and the Firedrake, stooping from the air, dashed with his burning horns and flaming feet slap into the body of the Remora.

Then there rose a steam so dreadful, such a white yet fiery vapour of heat, that no one who had not the prince's magic glass could have seen what happened. With horrible grunts and roars the Firedrake tried to burn his way right through the flat body of the Remora, and to chase him to his cleft in the rock. But the Remora, hissing terribly, and visibly melting away in places, yet held his ground; and the prince could see his cold white folds climbing slowly up the hoofs of the Firedrake—up and up, till they reached his knees, and the great burning beast roared like a hundred bulls with the pain. Then up the Firedrake leaped, and hovering on his fiery wings, he lighted in the midst of the Remora's back, and dashed into it with his horns. But the flat, cruel head writhed backwards, and, slowly bending over on itself, the wounded Remora slid greedily to fasten again on the limbs of the Firedrake.

Meanwhile, the prince, safe on his hill, was lunching on the loaf and the cold tongue he had brought with him.

"Go it, Remora! Go it, Firedrake! you're gaining. Give it him, Remora!" he shouted in the wildest excitement.

Nobody had ever seen such a battle; he had it all to himself, and he never enjoyed anything more. He hated the Remora so much, that he almost wished the Firedrake could beat it; for the Firedrake was the more natural beast of the pair. Still, he was alarmed when he saw that the vast flat body of the Remora was now slowly coiling backwards, backwards, into the cleft below the hill; while a thick wet mist showed how cruelly it had suffered. But the

Firedrake, too, was in an unhappy way; for his legs were now cold and black, his horns were black also, though his body, especially near the heart, glowed still like red-hot iron.

"Go it, Remora!" cried the prince: "his legs are giving way; he's groggy on his pins! One more effort, and he won't be able to move!"

Encouraged by this advice, the white, slippery Remora streamed out of his cavern again, more and more of him uncoiling, as if the mountain were quite full of him. He had lost strength, no doubt: for the steam and mist went up from him in clouds, and the hissing of his angry voice grew fainter; but so did the roars of the Firedrake. Presently they sounded more like groans; and at last the Remora slipped up his legs above the knees, and fastened on his very heart of fire. Then the Firedrake stood groaning like a black bull, knee-deep in snow; and still the Remora climbed and climbed.

"Go it now, Firedrake!" shouted the prince; for he knew that if the Remora won, it would be too cold for him to draw near the place, and cut off the Firedrake's head and tail.

"Go it, Drake! he's slackening!" cried the prince again; and the brave Firedrake made one last furious effort, and rising on his wings, dropped just on the spine of his enemy.

The wounded Remora curled back his head again on himself, and again crawled, steaming terribly, towards his enemy. But the struggle was too much for the gallant Remora. The flat, cruel head moved slower; the steam from his thousand wounds grew fiercer; and he gently breathed his last just as the Firedrake, too, fell over and lay exhausted. With one final roar, like the breath of a thousand furnaces, the Firedrake expired.

The prince, watching from the hill-top, could scarcely believe that these two *awful scourges of Nature*, which had so long devastated his country, were actually dead. But when he had looked on for half-an-hour, and only a river ran where the Remora had been, while the body of the Firedrake lay stark and cold, he hurried to the spot.

Drawing the sword of sharpness, he hacked off, at two blows, the iron head and the tail of the Firedrake. They were a weary weight to carry; but in a few strides of the shoes of swiftness he was at his castle, where he threw down his burden, and nearly fainted with excitement and fatigue.

But the castle clock struck half-past seven; dinner was at eight, and the poor prince crawled on hands and knees to the garret. Here he put on the wishing-cap; wished for a pint of champagne, a hot bath, and his best black velvet and diamond suit. In a moment these were provided; he bathed, dressed, drank a glass of wine, packed up the head and tail of

The Firedrake.

the Firedrake, sat down on the flying carpet, and knocked at the door of the English Ambassador as the clocks were striking eight in Gluckstein.

Punctuality is the politeness of princes; and a prince *is* polite when he is in love!

The prince was received at the door by a stout porter and led into the hall, where *several* butlers met him, and he laid the mortal remains of the Firedrake under the cover of the flying carpet.

Then he was led upstairs, and he made his bow to the pretty lady, who, of course, made him a magnificent courtesy. She seemed prettier and kinder than ever. The prince was so happy, that he never noticed how something went wrong about the dinner. The ambassador looked about, and seemed to miss someone, and spoke in a low voice to one of the servants, who answered also in a low voice, and what he said seemed to displease the ambassador. But the prince was so busy in talking to his lady, and in eating his dinner too, that he never observed anything unusual. He had *never* been at such a pleasant dinner!

CHAPTER XII.

A Terrible Misfortune.

WHEN the ladies left, and the prince and the other gentlemen were alone, the ambassador appeared more gloomy than ever. At last he took the prince into a corner, on pretence of showing him a rare statue.

"Does your royal highness not know," he asked, "that you are in considerable danger?"

"Still?" said the prince, thinking of the Firedrake.

The ambassador did not know what he meant, for *he* had never heard of the fight, but he answered gravely:

"Never more than now."

Then he showed the prince two proclamations, which had been posted all about the town.

Here is the first:

TO ALL LOYAL SUBJECTS.

Whereas,

Our eldest son, Prince Prigio, hath of late been guilty of several high crimes and misdemeanours.

First: By abandoning the post of danger against the Firedrake, whereby our beloved sons, Prince Alphonso and Prince Enrico, have perished, and been overdone by that monster.

Secondly: By attending an unseemly revel in the town of Gluckstein, where he brawled in the streets.

Thirdly: By trying to seduce away the hearts of our loyal subjects in that city, and to blow up a party against our crown and our peace.

This is to give warning,

That whoever consorts with, comforts, aids, or abets the said Prince Prigio, is thereby a partner in his treason; and

That a reward of Five Thousand Purses will be given to whomsoever brings the said prince, alive, to our Castle of Falkenstein.

Grognio R.

And here is the second proclamation:

Reward.
THE FIREDRAKE.

Whereas,

Our dominions have lately been devastated by a Firedrake (the *Salamander Furiosus* of Buffon);

This is to advise all,

That whosoever brings the horns and tail of the said Firedrake to our Castle of Falkenstein, shall receive Five Thousand Purses, the position of Crown Prince, with the usual perquisites, and the hand of the king's niece, the Lady Molinda.

Grognio R.

"H'm," said the prince; "I did not think his majesty wrote so well;" and he would have *liked* to say, "Don't you think we might join the ladies?"

"But, sir," said the ambassador, "the streets are lined with soldiers; and I know not how you have escaped them. *Here,* under my roof, you are safe for the moment; but a prolonged stay—excuse my inhospitality—could not but strain the harmonious relations which prevail between the Government of Pantouflia and that which I have the honour to represent."

"We don't want to fight; and no more, I think, do you," said the prince, smiling.

"Then how does your royal highness mean to treat the proclamations?"

"Why, by winning these ten thousand purses. I can tell you £1,000,000 is worth having," said the prince. "I'll deliver up the said prince, alive, at Falkenstein this very night; also the horns and tail of the said Firedrake. But I don't want to marry my Cousin Molly."

' May I remind your royal highness that Falkenstein is three hundred miles away? Moreover, my head butler, Benson, disappeared from the house before dinner, and I fear he went to warn Captain Kopzoffski that you are *here!*"

"That is nothing," said the prince; "but, my dear Lord Kelso, may I not have the pleasure of presenting Lady Rosalind with a little gift, a Philippine which I lost to her last night, merely the head and tail of a Firedrake which I stalked this morning?"

The ambassador was so astonished that he ran straight upstairs, forgetting his manners, and crying:

"Linda! Linda! come down at once; here's a surprise for you!"

Lady Rosalind came sweeping down, with a smile on her kind face. *She* guessed what it was, though the prince had said nothing about it at dinner.

"Lead the way, your royal highness!" cried the ambassador; and the prince offering Lady Rosalind his arm, went out into the hall, where he saw neither his carpet nor the horns and tail of the Firedrake!

He turned quite pale, and said:

"Will you kindly ask the servants where the little Persian prayer-rug and the parcel which I brought with me have been placed?"

Lord Kelso rang the bell, and in came all the servants, with William, the under-butler, at their head.

"William," said his lordship, "where have you put his royal highness's parcel and his carpet?"

"Please, your lordship," said William, "we think Benson have took them away with him."

"And where is Benson?"

"We don't know, your lordship. We think he have been come for!"

"Come for—by whom?"

William stammered, and seemed at a loss for a reply.

"Quick! answer! what do you know about it?"

William said at last, rather as if he were making a speech:

"Your royaliness, and my lords and ladies, it was like this. His royaliness comed in with a rug over his arm, and summat under it. And he lays it down on that there seat, and Thomas shows him into the droring-room. Then Benson says: 'Dinner'll be ready in five minutes; how tired I do feel!' Then he takes the libbuty of sitting hisself down on his royaliness's rug, and he says, asking your pardon, 'I've had about enough of service here. I'm about tired, and I thinks of bettering myself. I wish I was at the king's court, and butler.' But before the words was out of his mouth, off he flies like a shot through the open door, and his royaliness's parcel with him. I run to the door, and there he was, flying right hover the town, in a northerly direction. And that's all I know; for I would not tell a lie, not if it was

hever so. And me, and Thomas—as didn't see it,—and cook, we thinks as how Benson was come for. And cook says as she don't wonder at it, neither; for a grumblinger, more ill-conditioneder——"

"Thank you, William," said Lord Kelso; "that will do; you can go, for the present."

CHAPTER XIII.

Surprises.

THE prince said nothing, the ambassador said nothing, Lady Rosalind said never a word till they were in the drawing-room. It was a lovely warm evening, and the French windows were wide open on the balcony, which looked over the town and away north to the hills. Below them flowed the clear, green water of the Gluckthal. And still nobody said a word.

At last the prince spoke:

"This is a very strange story, Lord Kelso!"

"Very, sir!" said the ambassador.

"But true," added the prince; "at least, there is no reason in the nature of things why it shouldn't be true."

"I can hardly believe, sir, that the conduct of Benson, whom I always found a most respectable man, deserved——"

"That he should be 'come for,'" said the prince. "Oh, no; it was a mere accident, and might have happened to any of us who chanced to sit down on my carpet."

And then the prince told them, shortly, all

about it: how the carpet was one of a number of fairy properties, which had been given him at his christening; and how so long a time had gone by before he discovered them; and how, probably, the carpet had carried the butler where he had said he wanted to go—namely, to the king's Court at Falkenstein.

"It would not matter so much," added the prince, "only I had relied on making my peace with his majesty, my father, by aid of those horns and that tail. He was set on getting them; and if the Lady Rosalind had not expressed a wish for them, they would to-day have been in his possession."

"Oh, sir, you honour us too highly," murmured Lady Rosalind; and the prince blushed and said:

"Not at all! Impossible!"

Then, of course, the ambassador became quite certain that his daughter was admired by the crown prince, who was on bad terms with the king of the country; and a more uncomfortable position for an ambassador—however, they are used to them.

"What on earth am I to do with the young man?" he thought. "He can't stay here for ever; and without his carpet he can't get away, for the soldiers have orders to seize him as soon as he appears in the street. And in the meantime Benson will be pretending that *he* killed the Firedrake—for he must have got to Falkenstein by now,—and they will be for marrying him to the king's niece, and making my butler crown prince to the kingdom of Pantouflia! It is dreadful!"

Now all this time the prince was on the balcony, telling Lady Rosalind all about how he got the Firedrake done for, in the most modest way; for, as he said: "*I* didn't kill him: and it is really the Remora, poor fellow, who should marry Molly; but he's dead."

At this very moment there was a *whizz* in the air; something shot past them, and, through the open window, the king, the queen, Benson, and the mortal remains of the Firedrake were shot into the ambassador's drawing room!

CHAPTER XIV.

The King Explains.

THE first who recovered his voice and presence of mind was Benson.

"Did your lordship ring for coffee?" he asked, quietly; and when he was told "Yes," he bowed and withdrew, with majestic composure.

When he had gone, the prince threw himself at the king's feet, crying:

"Pardon, pardon, my liege!"

"Don't speak to me, sir!" answered the king, very angrily; and the poor prince threw himself at the feet of the queen.

But she took no notice of him whatever, no more than if he had been a fairy; and the prince heard her murmur, as she pinched her royal arms:

"I shall waken presently; this is nothing out of the way for a dream. Dr. Rumpfino ascribes it to imperfect nutrition."

All this time, the Lady Rosalind, as pale as a marble statue, was leaning against the side of the open window. The prince thought he could do nothing wiser than go and comfort her, so he induced her to sit down on a chair in the balcony,—for he felt that he was not wanted in the drawing-room;—and soon they were talking happily about the stars, which had begun to appear in the summer night.

Meanwhile, the ambassador had induced the king to take a seat; but there was no use in talking to the queen.

"It would be a miracle," she said to herself, "and miracles do not happen; therefore this has not happened. Presently, I shall wake up in my own bed at Falkenstein."

Now, Benson, William, and Thomas brought in the coffee, but the queen took no notice. When they went away, the rest of the company slipped off quietly, and the king was left alone with the ambassador; for the queen could hardly be said to count.

"You want to know all about it, I suppose?" said his majesty in a sulky voice. "Well, you have a right to it, and I shall tell you. We were just sitting down to dinner at Falkenstein, rather late,—hours get later every year, I think —when I heard a row in the premises, and the captain of the guard, Colonel McDougal, came and told us that a man had arrived with the horns and tail of the Firedrake, and was claiming the reward. Her majesty and I rose and went into the outer court, where we found, sitting on that carpet with a glass of beer in his hand, a respectable-looking upper servant,

whom I recognised as your butler. He informed us that he had just killed the beast, and showed us the horns and tail, sure enough; there they are! The tail is like the iron handle of a pump, but the horns are genuine. A pair were thrown up by a volcano, in my great-grandfather's time, Giglio I.* Excellent coffee this, of yours!"

The ambassador bowed.

"Well, we asked him *where* he killed the Firedrake, and he said in a garden near Gluckstein. Then he began to speak about the reward, and the 'perkisits,' as he called them, which it seems he had read about in my proclamation. Rather a neat thing; drew it up myself," added his majesty.

"Very much to the point," said the ambassador, wondering what the king was coming to.

"Glad you like it," said the king, much pleased. "Well, where was I? Oh, yes; your man said he had killed the creature in a garden, quite near Gluckstein. I didn't much like the whole affair: he is an alien, you see; and then there was my niece, Molinda—poor girl, *she* was certain to give trouble. Her heart is buried, if I may say so, with poor Alphonso. But the queen is a very remarkable woman —very remarkable——"

* The History of this Prince may be read in a treatise called *The Rose and the Ring*, by M. A. TITMARSH. London, 1855.

"Very!" said the ambassador, with perfect truth.

"'Caitiff!' she cries to your butler," his majesty went on; "'perjured knave, thou liest in thy throat! Gluckstein is a hundred leagues from here, and how sayest thou that thou slewest the monster, and camest hither in a few hours' space?' This had not occurred to me,—I am a plain king, but I at once saw the force of her majesty's argument. 'Yes,' said I; 'how did you manage it?' But he—your man, I mean—was not a bit put out. 'Why, your majesty,' says he, 'I just sat down on that there bit of carpet, wished I was here, and here *I ham*. And I'd be glad, having had the trouble,—and my time not being my own,—to see the colour of them perkisits, according to the proclamation.' On this her majesty grew more indignant, if possible. 'Nonsense!' she cried; 'a story out of the *Arabian Nights* is not suited for a modern public, and fails to win æsthetic credence.' These were her very words."

"Her majesty's expressions are ever choice and appropriate," said the ambassador.

"'Sit down there, on the carpet, knave,' she went on; 'ourself and consort'—meaning *me* —'will take our places by thy side, and *I* shall wish us in Gluckstein, at thy master's! When the experiment has failed, thy head shall from thy shoulders be shorn!' So your man merely said, 'Very well, mum,—your majesty, I mean,' and sat down. The queen took her place at the edge of the carpet; I sat between her and the butler, and she said, 'I wish I were in Gluckstein!' Then we rose, flew through the air at an astonishing pace, and here we are! So I suppose the rest of the butler's tale is true, which I regret; but a king's word is sacred, and he shall take the place of that sneak, Prigio. But as we left home before dinner, and as *yours* is over, may I request your lordship to believe that I should be delighted to take something cold?"

The ambassador at once ordered a sumptuous collation, to which the king did full justice; and his majesty was shown to the royal chamber, as he complained of fatigue. The queen accompanied him, remarking that she was sound asleep, but would waken presently. Neither of them said "Good-night" to the prince. Indeed, they did not see him again, for he was on the balcony with Lady Rosalind. They found a great deal to say to each other, and at last the prince asked her to be his wife; and she said that if the king and her father gave their permission—why, then she would! After this she went to bed; and the prince, who had not slept at all the night before, felt very sleepy also. But he knew that first he had something that must be done. So he went into the drawing-room, took his carpet, and wished to be—now where do you suppose? Beside the dead body of the Firedrake! There he was in a moment; and dreadful the body looked, lying stark and cold in the white moonshine. Then the prince cut off its four hoofs, put them in his wallet, and with these he flew back in a second, and met the ambassador just as he came from ushering the king to bed. Then the prince was shown his own room, where he locked up the hoofs, the carpet, the cap of darkness, and his other things in an iron box; and so he went to bed and dreamed of his Lady Rosalind.

CHAPTER XV.

The King's Cheque.

WHEN they all awakened next morning, their first ideas were confused. It is often confusing to wake in a strange bed, much more so when you have flown through the air, like the king, the queen, and Benson the butler. For her part, the queen was the most perplexed of all; for she did undeniably wake, and yet she was not at home, where she had expected to be. However, she was a determined woman, and stood to it that nothing unusual was occurring. The butler made up his mind to claim the crown princeship and the hand of the Lady Molinda; because, as he justly remarked to William, here was such a chance to better himself as might not soon come in his way again. As for the king, he was only anxious to get back to Falkenstein, and have the whole business settled in a constitutional manner. The ambassador was not sorry to get rid of the royal party; and it was proposed that they should all sit down on the flying carpet, and wish themselves at home again. But the queen would not hear of it:

she said it was childish and impossible; so the carriage was got ready for her, and she started without saying a word of good-bye to anyone. The king, Benson, and the prince were not so particular, and they simply flew back to Falkenstein in the usual way, arriving there at 11.35— a week before her majesty.

The king at once held a Court; the horns and tail of the monster were exhibited amidst general interest, and Benson and the prince were invited to state their claims.

Benson's evidence was taken first. He declined to say exactly where or how he killed the Firedrake. There might be more of them left, he remarked,—young ones, that would take a lot of killing,—and he refused to part with his secret. Only he claimed the reward, which was offered, if you remember, *not* to the man who killed the beast, but to him who brought its horns and tail. This was allowed by the lawyers present to be very sound law; and Benson was cheered by the courtiers, who decidedly preferred him to Prigio, and who, besides, thought he was going to be crown prince. As for Lady Molinda, she was torn by the most painful feelings; for, much as she hated Prigio, she could not bear the idea of marrying Benson. Yet one or the other choice seemed certain.

Unhappy lady! Perhaps no girl was ever more strangely beset by misfortune!

Prince Prigio was now called on to speak.

He admitted that the reward was offered for bringing the horns and tail, not for killing the monster. But were the king's *intentions* to go for nothing? When a subject only *meant* well, of course he had to suffer; but when a king said one thing, was he not to be supposed to have meant another? Any fellow with a waggon could *bring* the horns and tail; the difficult thing was to kill the monster. If Benson's claim was allowed, the royal prerogative of saying one thing and meaning something else was in danger.

On hearing this argument, the king so far forgot himself as to cry, "Bravo, well said!" and to clap his hands, whereon all the courtiers shouted and threw up their hats.

The prince then said that whoever had killed the monster could, of course, tell where to find him, and could bring his hoofs. He was ready to do this himself. Was Mr. Benson equally ready? On this being interpreted to him—for he did not speak Pantouflian—Benson grew pale with horror, but fell back on the proclamation. He had brought the horns and tail, and so he must have the perquisites, and the Lady Molinda!

The king's mind was so much confused by this time, that he determined to leave it to the Lady Molinda herself.

"Which of them will you have, my dear?" he asked, in a kind voice.

But poor Molinda merely cried. Then his majesty was almost *driven* to say that he would give the reward to whoever produced the hoofs by that day week. But no sooner had he said this than the prince brought them out of his wallet, and displayed them in open Court. This ended the case; and Benson, after being entertained with sherry and sandwiches in the steward's room, was sent back to his master. And I regret to say that his temper was not at all improved by his failure to better himself. On the contrary, he was unusually cross and disagreeable for several days; but we must, perhaps, make some allowance for his disappointment.

But if Benson was irritated, and suffered from the remarks of his fellow-servants, I do not think we can envy Prince Prigio. Here he was, restored to his position indeed, but by no means to *the royal favour*. For the king disliked him as much as ever, and was as angry as ever about the deaths of Enrico and Alphonso. Nay, he was even *more* angry; and, perhaps, not without reason. He called up Prigio before the whole Court, and thereon the courtiers cheered like anything, but the king cried:

"Silence! McDougal, drag the first man that shouts to the serpent-house in the zoological gardens, and lock him up with the rattlesnakes!"

After that the courtiers were very quiet.

"Prince," said the king as Prigio bowed before the throne, "you are restored to your position, because I cannot break my promise. But your base and malevolent nature is even more conspicuously manifest in your selfish success than in your previous dastardly contempt of duty. Why, confound you!" cried the king, dropping the high style in which he had been speaking, and becoming the *father*, not the *monarch*,—"why, if you *could* kill the Firedrake, did you let your poor little brothers go and be b—b—b—broiled? Eh! what do you say, you sneak? 'You didn't believe there *were* any Firedrakes?' That just comes of your eternal conceit and arrogance! If you were clever enough to kill the creature—and I admit that—you were clever enough to know that what everybody said must be true. 'You have not generally found it so?' Well, you *have* this time, and let it be a lesson to you; not that there is much comfort in that, for it is not likely you will ever have such another chance"—exactly the idea that had occurred to Benson.

Here the king wept, among the tears of the lord chief justice, the poet laureate (who had been awfully frightened when he heard of the rattlesnakes), the maids of honour, the chaplain royal, and everyone but Colonel McDougal, a Scottish soldier of fortune, who maintained a military reserve.

When his majesty had recovered, he said to Prigio (who had not been crying, he was too much absorbed):

"A king's word is his bond. Bring me a pen, somebody, and my cheque-book."

The royal cheque-book, bound in red morocco, was brought in by eight pages, with ink and a pen. His majesty then filled up and signed the following satisfactory document — (Ah! my children, how I wish Mr. Arrowsmith would do as much for *me!*):

No. W. $^{\text{o}}_{\text{B}}$ 961047.   FALKENSTEIN, *July* 10, 1768.

The Bank of Pantouflia.

FALKENSTEIN BRANCH.

Pay to *Prince Prigio* _____ or Order,
Ten Thousand Purses.

£1,000,000   *Grognio* R.

"There!" said his majesty, crossing his cheque and throwing sand over it, for blotting-paper had not yet been invented; "there, take *that*, and be off with you!"

Prince Prigio was respectfully but rapidly obeying his royal command, for he thought he had better cash the royal cheque as soon as possible, when his majesty yelled:

"Hi! here! come back! I forgot something; you've got to marry Molinda!"

CHAPTER XVI.

A Melancholy Chapter.

THE prince had gone some way, when the king called after him. How he wished he had the seven-league boots on, or that he had the cap of darkness in his pocket! If he had been so lucky, he would now have got back to Gluckstein, and crossed the border with Lady Rosalind. A million of money may not seem much, but a pair of young people who really love each other could live happily on less than the cheque he had in his pocket. However, the king shouted very loud, as he always did when he meant to be obeyed, and the prince sauntered slowly back again.

"Prigio!" said his majesty, "where were you off to? Don't you remember that this is your wedding-day? My proclamation offered, not only the money (which you have), but the hand of the Lady Molinda, which the Court chaplain will presently make your own. I congratulate you, sir; Molinda is a dear girl."

"I have the highest affection and esteem for my cousin, sir," said the prince, "but——"

"I'll never marry him!" cried poor Molinda, kneeling at the throne, where her streaming eyes and hair made a pretty and touching picture. "Never! I despise him!"

"I was about to say, sir," the prince went on, "that I cannot possibly have the pleasure of wedding my cousin."

"The family gibbet, I presume, is in good working order?" asked the king of the family executioner, a tall gaunt man in black and scarlet, who was only employed in the case of members of the blood royal.

"Never better, sire," said the man, bowing with more courtliness than his profession indicated.

"Very well," said the king; "Prince Prigio, you have your choice. *There* is the gallows, *here* is Lady Molinda. My duty is painful, but clear. A king's word cannot be broken. Molly, or the gibbet!"

The prince bowed respectfully to Lady Molinda:

"Madam, my cousin," said he, "your clemency will excuse my answer, and you will not misinterpret the apparent discourtesy of my conduct. I am compelled, most unwillingly, to slight your charms, and to select the Extreme Rigour of the Law. Executioner, lead on! Do your duty; for me, *Prigio est prêt;*"— for this was his motto, and meant that he was ready.

Poor Lady Molinda could not but be hurt by the prince's preference for death over marriage to her, little as she liked him.

"Is life, then, so worthless? and is Molinda so terrible a person that you prefer *those* arms," and she pointed to the gibbet, "to *these?*"—here she held out her own, which were very white, round and pretty: for Molinda was a good-hearted girl, she could not bear to see Prigio put to death; and then, perhaps, she reflected that there are worse positions than the queenship of Pantouflia. For Alphonso was gone—crying would not bring him back.

"Ah, Madam!" said the prince, "you are forgiving——"

"For *you* are brave!" said Molinda, feeling quite a respect for him.

"But neither your heart nor mine is ours to give. Since mine was another's, I understand too well the feeling of *yours!* Do not let us buy life at the price of happiness and honour."

Then, turning to the king the prince said:

"Sir, is there no way but by death or marriage? You say you cannot keep half only of your promise; and that, if I accept the reward, I must also unite myself with my unwilling cousin. Cannot the whole proclamation be annulled, and will you consider the bargain void if I tear up this flimsy scroll?"

And here the prince fluttered the cheque for £1,000,000 in the air.

For a moment the king was tempted; but then he said to himself:

"Never mind, it's only an extra penny on the income-tax." Then, "Keep your dross," he shouted, meaning the million; "but let *me* keep my promise. To chapel at once, or——" and he pointed to the executioner. "The word of a king of Pantouflia is sacred."

"And so is that of a crown prince," answered Prigio; "and *mine* is pledged to a lady."

"She shall be a mourning bride," cried the king savagely, " unless "—here he paused for a moment—"unless you bring me back Alphonso and Enrico, safe and well ! "

The prince thought for the space of a flash of lightning.

" I accept the alternative," he said, " if your majesty will grant me my conditions."

" Name them ! " said the king.

" Let me be transported to Gluckstein, left there unguarded, and if, in three days, I do not return with my brothers safe and well, your majesty shall be spared a cruel duty. Prigio of Pantouflia will perish by his own hand."

The king, whose mind did not work very quickly, took some minutes to think over it. Then he saw that by granting the prince's conditions, he would either recover his dear sons, or, at least, get rid of Prigio, without the unpleasantness of having him executed. For, though some kings have put their eldest sons to death, and most have wished to do so, they have never been better loved by the people for their Roman virtue.

" Honour bright ? " said the king at last.

" Honour bright ! " answered the prince, and for the first time in many months, the royal father and son shook hands.

" For you, madam," said Prigio in a stately

way to Lady Molinda," in less than a week I trust we shall be taking our vows at the same altar, and that the close of the ceremony which finds us cousins will leave us brother and sister."

Poor Molinda merely stared; for she could not imagine what he meant. In a moment he was gone; and having taken, by the king's permission, the flying carpet, he was back at the ambassador's house in Gluckstein.

CHAPTER XVII.

The Black Cat and the Brethren!

WHO was glad to see the prince, if it was not Lady Rosalind? The white roses of her cheeks turned to red roses in a moment, and then back to white again, they were so alarmed at the change. So the two went into the gardens together, and talked about a number of things; but at last the prince told her that, before three days were over, all would be well, or all would be over with him. For either he would have brought his brothers back, sound and well, to Falkenstein, or he would not survive his dishonour.

"It is no more than right," he said; "for had I gone first, neither of them would have been sent to meet the monster after I had fallen. And I *should* have fallen, dear Rosalind, if I had faced the Firedrake before I knew *you*."

Then when she asked him why, and what good she had done him, he told her all the story; and how, before he fell in love with her, he didn't believe in fairies, or Firedrakes, or caps of darkness, or anything nice and impossible, but only in horrid useless facts, and chemistry, and geology, and arithmetic, and mathematics, and even political economy. And the Firedrake would have made a mouthful of him, then.

So she was delighted when she heard this, almost as much delighted as she was afraid that he might fail in the most difficult adventure. For it was one thing to egg on a Remora to kill a Firedrake, and quite another to find the princes if they were alive, and restore them if they were dead!

But the prince said he had his plan, and he stayed that night at the ambassador's. Next morning he rose very early, before anyone else was up, that he might not have to say "Good-bye" to Lady Rosalind. Then he flew in a moment to the old lonely castle, where nobody went for fear of ghosts, ever since the Court retired to Falkenstein.

How still it was, how deserted; not a sign of life, and yet the prince was looking everywhere *for some living thing*. He hunted the castle through in vain, and then went out to the stable-yard; but all the dogs, of course, had been taken away, and the farmers had offered homes to the poultry. At last, stretched at full length in a sunny place, the prince found a very old, half-blind, miserable cat. The poor creature was lean, and its fur had fallen off in

POOR OLD FRANK

patches; it could no longer catch birds, nor even mice, and there was nobody to give it milk. But cats do not look far into the future; and this old black cat—Frank was his name— had got a breakfast somehow, and was happy in the sun. The prince stood and looked at him pityingly, and he thought that even a sick old cat was, in some ways, happier than most men.

"Well," said the prince at last, "he could not live long anyway, and it must be done. He will feel nothing."

Then he drew the sword of sharpness, and with one turn of his wrist cut the cat's head clean off.

It did not at once change into a beautiful young lady, as perhaps you expect; no, that was improbable, and, as the prince was in love already, would have been vastly inconvenient. The dead cat lay there, like any common cat.

Then the prince built up a heap of straw, with wood on it; and there he laid poor puss, and set fire to the pile. Very soon there was nothing of old black Frank left but ashes!

Then the prince ran upstairs to the fairy cupboard, his heart beating loudly with excitement. The sun was shining through the arrow-shot window; all the yellow motes were dancing in its rays. The light fell on the strange heaps of fairy things—talismans and spells. The prince hunted about here and there, and at last he discovered six ancient water-vessels of black leather, each with a silver plate on it, and on the plate letters engraved. This was what was written on the plates:

AQVA. DE. FONTE. LEONVM.*

"Thank heaven!" said the prince. "I thought they were sure to have brought it!"

Then he took one of the old black-leather bottles, and ran downstairs again to the place where he had burned the body of the poor old sick cat.

He opened the bottle, and poured a few drops of the water on the ashes and the dying embers.

Up there sprang a tall, white flame of fire, waving like a tongue of light; and forth from the heap jumped the most beautiful, strong, funny, black cat that ever was seen!

It was Frank as he had been in the vigour of his youth; and he knew the prince at once, and rubbed himself against him and purred.

The prince lifted up Frank and kissed his nose for joy; and a bright tear rolled down on Frank's face, and made him rub his nose with his paw in the most comical manner.

* Water from the Fountain of Lions.

Then the prince set him down, and he ran round and round after his tail; and, lastly, cocked his tail up, and marched proudly after the prince into the castle.

"Oh, Frank!" said Prince Prigio, "no cat since the time of Puss in Boots was ever so well taken care of as you shall be. For if the fairy water from the Fountain of Lions can bring *you* back to life—why, there is a chance for Alphonso and Enrico!"

Then Prigio bustled about, got ready some cold luncheon from the store-room, took all his fairy things that he was likely to need, sat down with them on the flying carpet, and wished himself at the mountain of the Firedrake.

"I have the king now," he said; "for if I can't find the ashes of my brothers, by Jove! I'll!——"

Do you know what he meant to do, if he could not find his brothers? Let every child guess.

Off he flew; and there he was in a second, just beside poor Alphonso's garden-engine. Then Prigio, seeing a little heap of grey ashes beside the engine, watered them with the fairy water; and up jumped Alphonso, as jolly as ever, his sword in his hand.

"Hullo, Prigio!" cried he; "are you come after the monster too? I've been asleep, and I had a kind of dream that he beat me. But the pair of us will tackle him. How is Molinda?"

"Prettier than ever," said Prigio; "but anxious about you. However, the Firedrake's dead and done for; so never mind him. But I left Enrico somewhere about. Just you sit down and wait a minute, till I fetch him."

The prince said this, because he did not wish Alphonso to know that he and Enrico had not had quite the best of it in the affair with the monster.

"All right, old fellow," says Alphonso; "but have you any luncheon with you? Never was so hungry in my life!"

Prince Prigio had thought of this, and he brought out some cold sausage (to which Alphonso was partial) and some bread, with which the younger prince expressed himself satisfied. Then Prigio went up the hill some way, first warning Alphonso *not* to sit on his carpet for fear of *accidents* like that which happened to Benson. In a hollow of the hill, sure enough there was the sword of Enrico, the diamonds of the hilt gleaming in the sun. And there was a little heap of grey ashes.

The prince poured a few drops of the water from the Fountain of Lions on them, and up, of course, jumped Enrico, just as Alphonso had done.

"Sleepy old chap you are, Enrico," said the prince; "but come on, Alphonso will have finished the grub unless we look smart."

So back they came, in time to get their share

of what was going; and they drank the Remora's very good health, when Prigio told them about the fight. But neither of them ever knew that they had been dead and done for; because Prigio invented a story that the mountain was enchanted, and that, as long as the Firedrake lived, everyone who came there fell asleep. He did tell them about the flying carpet, however, which of course did not much surprise them, because they had read all about it in the *Arabian Nights* and other historical works.

"And now I'll show you fun!" said Prigio; and he asked them both to take their seats on the carpet, and wished to be in the valley of the Remora.

There they were in a moment, among the old knights whom, if you remember, the Remora had frozen into stone. There was quite a troop of them, in all sorts of armour—Greek and Roman, and Knight Templars like Front de Bœuf and Brian du Bois Gilbert—all the brave warriors that had tried to fight the Remora since the world began.

Then Prigio gave each of his brothers some of the water in their caps, and told them to go round pouring a drop or two on each frozen knight. And as they did it, lo and behold! each knight came alive, with his horse, and lifted his sword and shouted:

"Long live Prince Prigio!"

in Greek, Latin, Egyptian, French, German, and Spanish,—all of which the prince perfectly understood, and spoke like a native.

So he marshalled them in order, and sent them off to ride to Falkenstein and cry:

"Prince Prigio is coming!"

Off they went, the horses' hoofs clattering, banners flying, sunshine glittering on the spear-points. Off they rode to Falkenstein; and when the king saw them come galloping in, I can tell you he had no more notion of hanging Prigio.

CHAPTER XVIII.

The Very Last.

THE princes returned to Gluckstein on the carpet, and went to the best inn, where they dined together and slept. Next morning they, and the ambassador, who had been told all the story, and Lady Rosalind, floated comfortably on the carpet, back to Falkenstein, where the king wept like anything on the shoulders of Alphonso and Enrico. They could not make out why he cried so, nor why Lady Molinda and Lady Kathleena cried; but soon they were all laughing and happy again. But then—would you believe he could be so mean?—he refused to keep his royal promise, and restore Prigio to his crown-princeship! Kings are like that.

But Prigio, very quietly asking for the head of the Firedrake, said he'd pour the magic water on *that*, and bring the Firedrake back to life again, unless his majesty behaved rightly. This threat properly frightened King Grognio, and he apologised. Then the king shook hands with Prigio in public, and thanked him, and said he was proud of him. As to Lady Rosalind, the old gentleman quite fell in love with her, and he sent at once to the Chaplain Royal to get into his surplice, and marry all the young people off at once, without waiting for wedding-cakes, and milliners, and all the rest of it.

Now, just as they were forming a procession to march into church, who should appear but the queen! Her majesty had been travelling by post all the time, and, luckily, had heard of none of the doings since Prigio, Benson, and the king left Gluckstein. I say *luckily* because if she *had* heard of them, she would not have believed a word of them. But when she saw Alphonso and Enrico, she was much pleased, and said:

"Naughty boys! Where have you been hiding? The king had some absurd story about your having been killed by a fabulous monster. Bah! don't tell *me*. I always said you would come back after a little trip—didn't I, Prigio?"

"Certainly, madam," said Prigio; "and I said so, too. Didn't I say so?" And all the courtiers cried: "Yes, you did;" but some added, to themselves, "He *always* says, 'Didn't I say so?'"

Then the queen was introduced to Lady Rosalind, and she said it was "rather a short engagement, but she supposed young people understood their own affairs best." And they do! So the three pairs were married, with the utmost rejoicings; and her majesty never, her whole life long, could be got to believe that anything unusual had occurred.

The honeymoon of Prince Prigio and the Crown Princess Rosalind was passed at the castle, where the prince had been deserted by the Court. But now it was delightfully fitted up; and Master Frank marched about the house with his tail in the air, as if the place belonged to him.

Now, on the second day of their honeymoon, the prince and princess were sitting in the garden together, and the prince said, "Are you *quite* happy, my dear?" and Rosalind said, "Yes; *quite*."

But the prince did not like the tone of her voice, and he said:

"No, there's something; do tell me what it is."

"Well," said Rosalind, putting her head on his shoulder, and speaking very low, "I want everybody to love you as much as I do. No, not quite so very much,—but I want them to like you. Now they *can't*, because they are afraid of you; for you are so awfully clever. Now, couldn't you take the wishing cap, and wish to be no cleverer than other people? Then everybody would like you!"

The prince thought a minute, then he said:

"Your will is law, my dear; anything to please you. Just wait a minute!"

Then he ran upstairs, for the last time, to the fairy garret, and he put on the wishing cap.

"No," thought he to himself, "I won't wish *that*. Every man has one secret from his wife, and this shall be mine."

Then he said aloud: "I WISH TO SEEM NO CLEVERER THAN OTHER PEOPLE."

Then he ran downstairs again, and the princess noticed a great difference in him (though, of course, there was really none at all), and so did everyone. For the prince remained as clever as ever he had been; but, as nobody observed it, he became the most popular prince, and finally the best-beloved king who had ever sat on the throne of Pantouflia.

But occasionally Rosalind would say, "I do believe, my dear, that you are really as clever as ever!"

And he *was!*

PRINCE RICARDO OF PANTOUFLIA

BEING THE ADVENTURES OF PRINCE PRIGIO'S SON.

PRINCE RICARDO

is

Dedicated

to

GUY CAMPBELL.

My dear Guy,

You wanted to know more about Prince Prigio, who won the Lady Rosalind, and killed the Firedrake and the Remora by aid of his Fairy gifts. Here you have some of his later adventures, and you will learn from this story the advantages of minding your book.

Yours always,

A Lang.

Introductory.

EXPLAINING MATTERS.

THERE may be children whose education has been so neglected that they have not read *Prince Prigio*. As this new story is about Prince Prigio's son, Ricardo, you are to learn that Prigio was the child and heir of Grognio, King of Pantouflia. The fairies gave the little Prince cleverness, beauty, courage; but one wicked fairy added, "You shall be *too* clever." His mother, the queen, hid away in a cupboard all the fairy presents,—the Sword of Sharpness, the Seven-League Boots, the Wishing Cap, and many other useful and delightful gifts, in which her Majesty did not believe! But after Prince Prigio had become universally disliked and deserted, because he was so very clever and conceited, he happened to find all the fairy presents in the old turret chamber where they had been thrown. By means of these he delivered his country from a dreadful Red-Hot Beast, called the Firedrake, and, in addition to many other triumphs, he married the good and beautiful Lady Rosalind. His love for her taught him not to be conceited, though he did not cease to be extremely clever and fond of reading.

When this new story begins the Prince has succeeded to the crown, on the death of King Grognio, and is unhappy about his own son, Prince Ricardo, who is not clever, and who hates books! The story tells of Ricardo's adventures: how he tried to bring back Prince Charlie to England, how he failed; how he dealt with the odious old Yellow Dwarf; how he was aided by the fair magician, the Princess Jaqueline; how they both fell into a dreadful trouble; how King Prigio saved them; and how Jaqueline's dear and royal papa was discovered; with the end of all these adventures. The moral of the story will easily be discovered by the youngest reader, or, if not, it does not much matter.

CHAPTER I.

The Troubles of King Prigio.

"'M sure I don't know what to do with that boy!" said King Prigio of Pantouflia.

"If *you* don't know, my dear," said Queen Rosalind, his illustrious consort, "I can't see what is to be done. You are so clever."

The king and queen were sitting in the royal library, of which the shelves were full of the most delightful fairy books in all languages, all equally familiar to

King Prigio. The queen could not read most of them herself, but the king used to read them aloud to her. A good many years had passed — seventeen, in fact — since Queen Rosalind was married, but you would not think it to look at her. Her grey eyes were as kind and soft and beautiful, her dark hair as dark, and her pretty colour as like a white rose blushing, as on the day when she was a bride. And she was as fond of the king as when he was only Prince Prigio, and he was as fond of her as on the night when he first met her at the ball.

"No, I don't know what to do with Dick," said the king.

He meant his son, Prince Ricardo, but he called him Dick in private.

"I believe it's the fault of his education," his Majesty went on. "We have not brought him up rightly. These fairy books are at the bottom of his provoking behaviour," and he glanced round the shelves. "Now, when *I* was a boy, my dear mother tried to prevent me from reading fairy books, because she did not believe in fairies."

"But she was wrong, you know," said the queen. "Why, if it had not been for all these fairy presents, the Cap of Darkness and all the rest of them, you never could have killed the Fire-beast and the Ice-beast, and — you never could have married me," the queen added, in a happy whisper, blushing beautifully, for that was a foolish habit of hers.

"It is quite true," said the king, "and therefore I thought it best to bring Dick up on fairy books, that he might know what is right, and have no nonsense about him. But perhaps the thing has been overdone; at all events, it is not a success. I wonder if fathers and sons will ever understand each other, and get on well together? There was my poor father, King Grognio, he wanted me to take to adventures, like other princes, fighting Firedrakes, and so forth; and I did not care for it, till *you* set me on," and he looked very kindly at her Majesty. "And now, here's Dick," the monarch continued, "I can't hold him back. He is always after a giant, or a dragon, or a magician, as the case may be; he will certainly be ploughed for his examination at College. Never opens a book. What does he care, off after every adventure he can hear about? An idle, restless youth! Ah, my poor country, when I am gone, what may not be your misfortunes under Ricardo!"

Here his Majesty sighed, and seemed plunged in thought.

"But you are not going yet, my dear," said the queen. "Why you are not forty! And young people will be young people. You were quite proud when poor Dick came home with his first brace of gigantic fierce birds, killed off his own sword, and with such a pretty princess he had rescued—dear Jaqueline? I'm sure she is like a daughter to me. I cannot do without her."

"I wish she were a daughter-in-law; I wish Dick would take a fancy to marry her," said the king. "A nicer girl I never saw."

"And so accomplished," added Queen Rosalind. "That girl can turn herself into anything—a mouse, a fly, a lion, a wheelbarrow, a church! I never knew such talent for magic. Of course she had the *best* of teachers, the Fairy Paribanou herself; but very few girls, in our time, devote so many hours to *practice* as dear Jaqueline. Even now, when she is out of the schoolroom, she still practises her scales. I saw her turning little Dollie into a fish and back again in the bath-room last night. The child was delighted."

In these times, you must know, princesses learned magic, just as they learn the piano nowadays; but they had their music lessons too, dancing, calisthenics, and the use of the globes.

"Yes, she's a dear, good girl," said the king; "yet she looks melancholy. I believe, myself, that if Ricardo asked her to marry him, she would not say 'No.' But that's just one of the things I object to most in Dick. Round the world he goes, rescuing ladies from every kind of horror—from dragons, giants, cannibals, magicians; and then, when a girl naturally expects to be married to him, as is usual, off he rides! He has no more heart than a flounder. Why, at his age I——"

"At his age, my dear, you were so hard-hearted that you were quite a proverb. Why, I have been told that you used to ask girls dreadful puzzling questions, like 'Who was Cæsar Borgia?' 'What do you know of Edwin and Morcar?' and so on."

"I had not seen *you* then," said the king.

"And Ricardo has not seen *her*, whoever she may be. Besides, he can't possibly marry all of them. And I think a girl should consider herself lucky if she is saved from a dragon or a giant, without expecting to be married next day."

"Perhaps; but it is usual," said the king, "and their families expect it, and keep sending ambassadors to know what Dick's intentions are. I would not mind it all so very much if he killed the monsters off his own sword, as he did that first brace, in fair fight. But ever since he found his way into that closet where the fairy presents lie, everything has been made too easy for him. It is a royal road to glory, or giant-slaying made easy. In his Cap of Darkness a poor brute of a dragon can't see him. In his Shoes of Swiftness the giants can't catch him. His Sword of Sharpness would cut any oak asunder at a blow!"

"But you were very glad of them when you

made the Ice-beast and the Fire-beast fight and kill each other," said the queen.

"Yes, my dear; but it wanted some wit, if I may say so, to do *that*, and Dick just goes at it hammer and tongs: anybody could do it. It's *intellect* I miss in Ricardo. How am I to know whether he could make a good fight for it without all these fairy things? I wonder what the young rogue is about to-day? He'll be late for dinner, as usual, I daresay. I can't stand want of punctuality at meals," remarked his Majesty, which is a sign that he was growing old after all; for where is the fun of being expected always to come home in time for dinner when, perhaps, you are fishing, and the trout are rising splendidly?

"Young people will be young people," said the queen. "If you are anxious about him, why don't you look for him in the magic crystal?"

Now the magic crystal was a fairy present, a great ball of glass in which, if you looked, you saw the person you wanted to see, and what he was doing, however far away he might be, if he was on the earth at all.*

"I'll just take a look at it," said the king; "it only wants three-quarters of an hour to dinner-time."

His Majesty rose, and walked to the crystal

---

* You can buy these glasses now from the Psychical Society, at half-a-crown and upwards.

globe, which was in a stand, like other globes. He stared into it, he turned it round and round, and Queen Rosalind saw him grow quite pale as he gazed.

"I don't see him anywhere," said the king, "and I have looked everywhere. I do hope nothing has happened to the boy. He is so careless. If he dropped his Cap of Darkness in a fight with a giant, why who knows what might occur?"

"Oh, 'Gio, how you frighten me!" said the queen.

King Prigio was still turning the crystal globe.

"Stop!" he cried; "I see a beautiful princess, fastened by iron chains to a rock beside the sea, in a lonely place. They must have fixed her up as a sacrifice to a sea-monster, like what's-her-name."

This proves how anxious he was, or, being so clever and learned, he would have remembered that her name was Andromeda.

"I bet Dick is not far off, where there is an adventure on hand. But where on earth can he be? . . . My word!" suddenly exclaimed the monarch, in obvious excitement.

"What is it, dear?" cried the queen, with all the anxiety of a mother.

"Why, the sea where the girl is, has turned all red as blood!" exclaimed the king. "Now it is all being churned up by the tail of a tremendous monster. He is a whopper! He's coming on shore; the girl is fainting. He's out on shore! He is extremely poorly, blood rushing from his open jaws. He's dying! And, hooray! here's Dick coming out of his enormous mouth, all in armour set with sharp spikes, and a sword in his hand. He's covered with blood, but he's well and hearty. He must have been swallowed by the brute, and cut him up inside. Now he's cutting the beast's head off. Now he's gone to the princess; a very neat bow he has made her. Dick's manners are positively improving! Now he's cutting her iron chains off with the Sword of Sharpness. And now he's made her another bow, and he's actually taking leave of her. Poor thing! How disappointed she is looking. And she's so pretty, too. I say, Rosalind, shall I shout to him through the magic horn, and tell him to bring her home here, on the magic carpet?"

"I think not, dear; the palace is quite full," said the queen. But the real reason was that she wanted Ricardo to marry her favourite Princess Jaqueline, and she did not wish the new princess to come in the way.

"As you like," said the king, who knew what was in her mind very well. "Besides, I see her own people coming for her. I'm sorry for her, but it can't be helped, and Dick is half-way home by now on the Shoes of Swiftness. I daresay he will not keep dinner waiting after all. But what a fright the boy has given me!"

At this moment a whirring in the air and a joyous shout were heard. It was Prince Ricardo flying home on his Seven-league Boots.

"Hi, Ross!" he shouted, "just weigh this beast's head. I've had a splendid day with a sea-monster. Get the head stuffed, will you? We'll have it set up in the billiard-room."

"Yes, Master Dick — I mean your Royal Highness," said Ross, a Highland keeper, who had not previously been employed by a Reigning Family. "It's a fine head, whatever," he added, meditatively.

Prince Ricardo now came beneath the library window, and gave his parents a brief account of his adventure.

"I picked the monster up early in the morning," he said, "through the magic telescope, father."

"What country was he in?" said the king.

"The country people whom I met called it Ethiopia. They were niggers."

"And in what part of the globe is Ethiopia, Ricardo?"

"Oh! I don't know. Asia, perhaps," answered the prince.

The king groaned.

"That boy will *never* understand our foreign relations. Ethiopia in Asia!" he said to him-

"It's a fine head, whatever."

self, but he did not choose to make any remark at the moment.

The prince ran upstairs to dress. On the stairs he met the Princess Jaqueline.

"Oh, Dick! are you hurt?" she said, turning very pale.

"No, not I; but the monster is. I had a capital day, Jack; rescued a princess, too."

"Was she—was she very pretty, Dick?"

"Oh! I don't know. Pretty enough, I daresay. Much like other girls. Why, you look quite white! What's the matter? Now you look all right again;" for, indeed, the Princess Jaqueline was blushing.

"I must dress. I'm ever so late," he said, hurrying upstairs; and the princess, with a little sigh, went down to the royal drawing-room.

CHAPTER II.

Princess Jaqueline Drinks the Moon.

WHEN dinner was over and the ladies had left the room, the king tried to *speak seriously* to Prince Ricardo. This was a thing which he disliked doing very much.

"There's very little use in preaching," his Majesty used to say, "to a man, or rather a boy, of another generation. My taste was for books; I only took to adventures because I was obliged to do it. Dick's taste is for adventures; I only wish some accident would make him take to books. But everyone must get his experience for himself; and when he has got it, he is lucky if it is not too late. I wish I could see him in love with some nice girl, who would keep him at home."

The king did not expect much from talking seriously to Dick. However, he began by asking questions about the day's sport, which Ricardo answered with modesty. Then his Majesty observed that, from all he had ever read or heard, he believed Ethiopia, where the fight was, to be in Africa, not in Asia.

"I really wish, Ricardo, that you would attend to your geography a little more. It is most necessary to a soldier that he should know where his enemy is, and if he has to fight the Dutch, for instance, not to start with his army for Central Asia."

"I could always spot them through the magic glass, father," said Dick; "it saves such a lot of trouble. I hate geography."

"But the glass might be lost or broken, or the Fairies might take it away, and then where are you?"

"Oh, *you* would know where to go, or Mr. Belsham."

Now Mr. Belsham was his tutor, from Oxford.

"But I shall not always be here, and when I die——"

"Don't talk of dying, sire," said Dick. "Why, you are not so very old; you may live for years yet. Besides, I can't stand the notion. You must live for ever!"

"That sentiment is unusual in a Crown Prince," thought the king; but he was pleased for all that.

"Well, to oblige you, I'll try to struggle against old age," he said; "but there are always accidents. Now, Dick, like a good fellow, and to please me, work hard all to-morrow till the afternoon. I'll come in and help you. And there's always a splendid evening rise of trout in the lake just now, so you can have your play after your work. You'll enjoy it more, and I daresay you are tired after a long day with the big game. It used to tire me, I remember."

"I *am* rather tired," said Dick; and indeed he looked a little pale, for a day in the inside of a gigantic sea-monster is fatiguing, from the heat and want of fresh air which are usually found in such places. "I think I'll turn in; good-night, my dear old governor," he said, in an affectionate manner, though he was not usually given to many words.

Then he went and kissed his mother and the Princess Jaqueline, whom he engaged to row him on the lake next evening, while he fished.

"And don't you go muffing them with the landing-net, Jack, as you generally do," said his Royal Highness, as he lit his bedroom candle.

"I wish he would not call me Jack," said the princess to the queen.

"It's better than Lina, my dear," said her Majesty, who in late life had become fond of her little joke; "that always sounds as if someone else was fatter,—and I hope there is not someone else."

The princess was silent, and fixed her eyes on her book.

Presently the king came in, and played a game with Lina at picquet. When they were all going to bed, he said:

"Just come into the study, Lina. I want you to write a few letters for me."

The princess followed him and took her seat at the writing table. The letters were very short. One was to Herr Schnipp, tailor to the king and royal family; another was to the royal swordmaker, another to the bootmaker, another to the optician, another to the tradesman who supplied the august family with carpets and rugs, another to his Majesty's hatter. They were all summoned to be at the palace early next morning. Then his Majesty yawned, apologised, and went to bed.

The princess also went to her room, or bower as it was then called, but not to sleep.

She was unhappy that Dick did not satisfy his father, and that he was so careless, and also about other things.

"And why does the king want all these tailors and hatters so suddenly, telescope-makers and swordmakers and shoemakers, too?" she asked herself, as she stood at the window watching the moon.

"I *could* find out. I could turn myself into

a dog or a cat, and go into the room where he is giving his orders. But that is awkward, for when the servants see Rip " (that was the dog) " in two places at once, they begin to think the palace is haunted, and it makes people talk. Besides, I know it is wrong to listen to what one is not meant to hear. It is often difficult to be a magician and a good girl. The temptations are so strong, stronger than most people allow for."

So she remained, with the moon shining on her pretty yellow hair and her white dress, wondering what the king intended to do, and whether it was something that Dick would not like.

"How stupid of me," she said at length, "after all the lessons I have had. Why, I can *drink the moon!*"

Now, this is a way of knowing what anyone else is thinking of and intends to do, for the moon sees and knows everything. Whether it is *quite fair* is another matter; but, at all events, it is not *listening*. And anyone may see that, if you are a magician, like the Princess Jaqueline, a great many difficult questions as to what is right and wrong at once occur which do not trouble other people. King Prigio's secret, why he sent for the tailor and the other people, was his own secret. The princess decided that she would not find it out by turning herself into Rip or the cat (whose name was Semiramis), and, so far, she was quite right. But she was very young, and it never occurred to her that it was just as wrong to find out what the king meant by *drinking the moon* as by listening in disguise. As she grew older she learned to know better; but this is just the danger of teaching young girls magic, and for that very reason it has been given up in most countries.

However, the princess did not think about right and wrong, unluckily. She went to the bookcase and took down her *Cornelius Agrippa*, in one great tall black volume, with silver clasps which nobody else could open; for, as the princess said, there are books which it would never do to leave lying about where the servants or anybody could read them. Nobody could undo the clasps, however strong or clever he might be; but the princess just breathed on them and made a sign, and the book flew open at the right place—Book IV., chapter vi., about the middle of page 576.

The magic spell was in Latin, of course; but the princess knew Latin very well, and soon she had the magic song by heart. Then she closed the book and put it back on the shelf. Then she threw open the window and drew back the curtains, and put out all the lights except two scented candles that burned with a white fire under a round mirror with a silver frame, opposite the window. And into that mirror the moon shone white and full, filling all the space of it, so that the room was steeped in a strange silver light. Now the whole room seemed to sway gently, waving and trembling; and as it trembled it sounded and rang with a low silver music, as if it were filled with the waves of the sea.

Then the princess took a great silver basin, covered with strange black signs and figures raised in the silver. She poured water into the basin, and as she poured it she sang the magic spell from the Latin book. It was something like this, in English:

> "Oh Lady Moon, on the waters riding,
>   On shining waters, in silver sheen,
> Show me the secret the heart is hiding,
>   Show me the truth of the thought, oh Queen!
>
> "Oh waters white, where the moon is riding,
>   That knows what shall be and what has been,
> Tell me the secret the heart is hiding,
>   Wash me the truth of it, clear and clean!"

As she sang the water in the silver basin foamed and bubbled, and then fell still again; and the princess knelt in the middle of the room, and the moon and the white light from the mirror of the moon fell in the water.

Then the princess raised the basin, and stooped her mouth to it and drank the water, spilling a few drops, and so she *drank the moon* and the knowledge of the moon. Then the moon was darkened without a cloud, and there was darkness in the sky for a time, and all the dogs

The Princess drinks the Moon.

in the world began to howl. When the moon shone again, the princess rose and put out the two white lights, and drew the curtains; and presently she went to bed.

"Now I know all about it," she said. "It is clever; everything the king does is clever, and he is so kind that I daresay he does not mean any harm. But it seems a cruel trick to play on poor Ricardo. However, Jaqueline is on the watch, and I'll show them a girl can do more than people think,"—as, indeed, she could.

After meditating in this way, the princess fell asleep, and did not waken till her maid came to call her.

"Oh! your Royal Highness, what's this on the floor?" said the faithful Rosina, as she was arranging the princess's things for her to get up.

"Why, what is it?" asked the princess.

"Ever so many—four, five, six, seven—little shining drops of silver lying on the carpet, as if they had melted and fallen there!"

"They have not hurt the carpet?" said the princess. "Oh dear! the queen won't be pleased at all. It was a little chemical experiment I was trying last night."

But she knew very well that she must have dropped seven drops of the enchanted water.

"No, your Royal Highness, the carpet is not harmed," said Rosina; "only your Royal Highness should do these things in the laboratory. Her Majesty has often spoke about it."

"You are quite right," said the princess; "but as there is no harm done, we'll say nothing about it this time. And, Rosina, you may keep the silver drops for yourself."

"Your Royal Highness is always very kind," said Rosina, which was true; but how much better and wiser it is not to *begin* to deceive! We never know how far we may be carried, and so Jaqueline found out.

For when she went down to breakfast, there was the king in a great state of excitement, for him.

"It's *most* extraordinary," said his Majesty.

"What is?" asked the queen.

"Why, didn't you notice it? No, you had gone to bed before it happened. But I was taking a walk in the moonlight, on the balcony, and I observed it carefully."

"Observed what, my dear?" asked the queen, who was pouring out the tea.

"Didn't you see it, Dick? Late as usual, you young dog!" the king remarked as Ricardo entered the room.

"See what, sir?" said Dick.

"Oh, you were asleep hours before, now I think of it! But it was *the* most extraordinary thing, an unpredicted eclipse of the moon! You must have noticed it, Jaqueline; you sat up later. How the dogs howled!"

"No; I mean yes," murmured poor Jaqueline, who of course had caused the whole affair by her magic arts, but who had forgotten, in the excitement of the moment, that an eclipse of the moon, especially if entirely unexpected, is likely to attract very general attention. Jaqueline could not bear to tell a fib, especially to a king who had been so kind to her; besides, fibbing would not alter the facts.

"Yes, I did see it," she admitted, blushing.
"Had it not been predicted?"

"Not a word about it whispered anywhere," said his Majesty. "I looked up the almanack at once. It is the most extraordinary thing I ever saw, and I've seen a good many."

"The astronomers must be duffers," said Prince Ricardo. "I never thought there was much in physical science of any sort; most dreary stuff. Why, they say the earth goes round the sun, whereas any fool can see it is just the other way on."

King Prigio was struck aghast by these sentiments in the mouth of his son and heir, the hope of Pantouflia. But what was the king to say in reply? The astronomers of Pantouflia, who conceived that they knew a great deal, had certainly been taken by surprise this time. Indeed, they have not yet satisfactorily explained this eclipse of the moon, though they have written volumes about it.

"Why, it may be the sun next!" exclaimed his Majesty. "Anything may happen. The very laws of gravitation themselves may go askew!"

At this moment the butler, William, who had been in the queen's family when she was a girl, entered, and announced:

"Some of the royal tradesmen, by appointment, to see your Majesty."

So the king, who had scarcely eaten any breakfast, much to the annoyance of the queen, who was not agitated by eclipses, went out and joined the tailors and the rest of them.

CHAPTER III.

The Adventure of the Shopkeepers.

DICK went on with his breakfast. He ate cold pastry, and poached eggs, and ham, and rolls, and raspberry jam, and hot cakes; and he drank two cups of coffee. Meanwhile the king had joined the tradesmen who attended by his orders. They were all met in the royal study, where the king made them a most splendid bow, and requested them to be seated. But they declined to sit in his sacred presence, and the king observed that, in that case he must stand up.

"I have invited you here, gentlemen," he said, "on a matter of merely private importance, but I must request that you will be entirely silent as to the nature of your duties. It is difficult, I know, not to talk about one's work, but in this instance I am sure you will oblige me."

"Your Majesty has only to command," said Herr Schnipp. "There have been monarchs, in neighbouring kingdoms, who would have cut off all our heads after we had done a bit of secret business; but the merest word of your Majesty is law to your loving subjects."

The other merchants murmured assent, for King Prigio was really liked by his people. He was always good-tempered and polite. He never went to war with anybody. He spent most of the royal income on public objects, and of course there were scarcely any taxes to speak of. Moreover, he had abolished what is called compulsory education, or making everybody go to school whether he likes it or not; a most mischievous and tyrannical measure! "A fellow who can't teach himself to read," said the king, "is not worth teaching."

For all these reasons, and because they were so fond of the queen, his subjects were ready to do anything in reason for King Prigio.

Only one tradesman, bowing very deep and blushing very much, said:

"Your Majesty, will you hear me for one moment?"

"For an hour, with pleasure, Herr Schmidt," said the monarch.

"It is an untradesman-like and an unusual thing to decline an order; and if your Majesty asked for my heart's blood, I am ready to shed it, not to speak of anything in the line of my business—namely, boot and shoe making. But keep a secret from my wife, I fairly own to your Majesty that I can *not*."

Herr Schmidt went down on his knees and wept.

"Rise, Herr Schmidt," said the king, taking him by the hand. "A more honourable and chivalrous confession of an amiable weakness, if it is to be called a weakness, I never heard. Sir, you have been true to your honour and your prince, in face of what few men can bear, the chance of ridicule. There is no one here, I hope, but respects and will keep the secret of Herr Schmidt's confession?"

The assembled shopkeepers could scarcely refrain from tears.

"Long live King Prigio the Good!" they exclaimed, and vowed that everything should be kept dark.

"Indeed, sire," said the swordmaker, "all the rest of us are bachelors."

"That is none the worse for my purpose, gentlemen," said his Majesty; "but I trust that you will not long deprive me of sons and subjects worthy to succeed to such fathers. And now, if Herr Schmidt will kindly find his way to the buttery, where refreshments are ready, I shall have the pleasure of conducting you to the scene of your labours."

Thus speaking, the king, with another magni-

Herr Schmidt went down on his knees.

ficent bow, led the way upstairs to a little turret-room, in a deserted part of the palace. Bidding the tradesmen enter, he showed them a large collection of miscellaneous things: an old cap or two, a pair of boots of a sort long out of fashion, an old broadsword, a shabby old Persian rug, an ivory spyglass, and other articles. These were, in fact, the fairy presents, which had been given to the king at his christening, and by aid of which (and his natural acuteness) he had, in his youth, succeeded in many remarkable adventures.

The caps were the Wishing Cap and the Cap of Darkness. The rug was the famous carpet which carried its owner through the air wherever he wished to go. The sword was the Sword of Sharpness. The ivory glass showed you anyone you wanted to see, however far off. The boots were the Seven-league Boots, which Hop-o'-my-Thumb stole from the Ogre about 1697. There were other valuable objects, but these were the most useful and celebrated. Of course the king did not tell the tradesmen what they were.

"Now, gentlemen," said his Majesty, "you see these old things. For reasons which I must ask you to excuse me for keeping to myself, I wish you to provide me with objects exactly and precisely similar to these, with all the look of age."

The tradesmen examined the objects, each choosing that in his own line of business.

"As to the sword, sire," said the cutler, "it is an Andrea Ferrara, a fine old blade. By a lucky accident, I happen to have one at home, in a small collection of ancient weapons, exactly like it. This evening it shall be at your Majesty's disposal."

"Perhaps, Herr Schnitzler, you will kindly write an order for it, as I wish no one of you to leave the palace, if you can conveniently stay, till your business is finished."

"With pleasure, your Majesty," says the cutler.

"As to the old rug," said the upholsterer, "I have a Persian one quite identical with it at home, at your Majesty's service."

"Then you can do like Herr Schnitzler," who was the cutler.

"And I," said the hatter, "have two old caps just like these, part of a bankrupt theatrical stock."

"We are most fortunate," said the king. "The boots, now I come to think of it, are unimportant, at least for the present. Perhaps we can borrow a pair from the theatre."

"As for the glass," said the optician, "if your Majesty will allow me to take it home with me——"

"I am afraid I cannot part with it," said the king; "but that, too, is unimportant, or not very pressing."

Then he called for a servant, to order luncheon for the shopkeepers, and paper for them to write their orders on. But no one was within hearing, and in that very old part of the palace there were no bells.

"Just pardon me for an instant, while I run downstairs," said his Majesty; "and, it seems a strange thing to ask, but may I advise you not to sit down on that carpet? I have a reason for it."

In fact, he was afraid that someone might sit down on it, and wish he was somewhere else, and be carried away, as was the nature of the carpet.

King Prigio was not absent a minute, for he met William on the stairs; but when he came back, there was not one single person in the turret-room!

"Where on earth are they?" cried the king, rushing through all the rooms in that part of the castle. He shouted for them, and looked everywhere; but there was not a trace of tailor, hatter, optician, swordmaker, upholsterer.

The king hastened to a window over the gate, and saw the sentinels on duty.

"Hi!" he called.

And the sentinels turned round, looked up, and saluted.

"Have you seen anyone go out?" he cried.

"No one, sire," answered the soldiers.

The king, who began to guess what had happened, hurried back to the turret-room.

There were all the tradesmen with parcels under their arms.

"What means this, gentlemen?" said his Majesty, severely. "For what reason did you leave the room without my permission?"

They all knelt down, humbly imploring his compassion.

"Get up, you donkeys!" said the king, forgetting his politeness. "Get up, and tell me where you have been hiding yourselves."

The hatter came forward, and said:

"Sire, you will not believe me; indeed, I can scarcely believe it myself!"

"Nor none of us can't," said the swordmaker. "We have been home, and brought the articles. All orders executed with punctuality and dispatch," he added, quoting his own advertisement without thinking of it.

On this the swordmaker took out and exhibited the Andrea Ferrara blade, which was exactly like the Sword of Sharpness.

The upholsterer undid his parcel, and there was a Persian rug, which no one could tell from the magical carpet.

The hatter was fumbling with the string of his parcel, when he suddenly remembered, what the king in his astonishment had not noticed, that he had a cap on himself. He pulled it off in a hurry, and the king at once saw that it was his Wishing Cap, and understood all about the affair. The hatter, in his absence, had tried on the Wishing Cap, and had wished that he himself and his friends were all at home and back again with their wares at the palace. And what he wished happened, of course, as was natural.

In a moment the king saw how much talk this business would produce in the country, and he decided on the best way to stop it.

Seizing the Wishing Cap, he put it on, wished all the tradesmen, including the shoemaker, back in the town at their shops, and also wished that none of them should remember anything about the whole affair.

In a moment he was alone in the turret-room. As for the shopkeepers, they had a kind of idea that they had dreamed something odd; but, as it went no further, of course they did not talk about it, and nobody was any the wiser.

"Owl that I am!" said King Prigio to himself. "I might have better wished for a complete set of sham fairy things which would not work. It would have saved a great deal of trouble; but I am so much out of the habit of using the cap, that I never thought of it. However, what I have got will do very well."

Then, putting on the Cap of Darkness, that nobody might see him, he carried all the *real* fairy articles away, except the Seven-league Boots, to his own room, where he locked them up, leaving in their place the sham Wishing

Cap, the sham Cap of Darkness, the sham Sword of Sharpness, and the carpet which was not a magic carpet at all.

His idea was, of course, that Ricardo would start on an expedition confiding in his fairy things, and he would find that they did not act. Then he would be left to his own cleverness and courage to get him out of the scrape. That would teach him, thought the king, to depend on himself, and to set a proper value on cleverness and learning, and minding his book.

Of course he might have locked the things up, and forbidden Ricardo to touch them, but that might have seemed harsh. And, as you may easily imagine, with all the powers at his command, the king fancied he could easily rescue Ricardo from any very serious danger at the hands of giants or magicians or monsters. He only wanted to give him a fright or two, and make him respect the judgment of older and wiser people than himself.

CHAPTER IV.

Two Lectures.

FOR several days Prince Ricardo minded his books, and, according to his tutors, made considerable progress in polite learning. Perhaps he ought not to be praised too highly for this, because, in fact, he saw no means of distinguishing himself by adventures just at that time. Every morning he would climb the turret and sweep the horizon, and even *much* beyond the horizon, with the ivory spy-glass. But look as he would, he saw no monsters preying on human-kind anywhere, nor princesses in distress. To be sure he saw plenty of poor people in distress, and, being a good-hearted, though careless, lad, Dick would occasionally fly off with the Purse of Fortunatus in his pocket, and give them as much money as they needed — it cost him nothing. But this was not the kind of adventure which he enjoyed. Dragons for his money!

One day the Princess Jaqueline took a curious plan of showing Ricardo how little interest, after all, there is in performing the most wonderful exploits without any real difficulty or danger. They were drifting before a light breeze on a hill lake; Ricardo was fishing, and Jaqueline was sculling a stroke now and then, just to keep the boat right with the wind. Ricardo had very bad sport, when suddenly the trout began to rise all over the lake. Dick got excited, and stumbled about the boat from stern to bow, tripping over Jaqueline's feet, and nearly upsetting the vessel in his hurry to throw his flies over every trout he saw feeding. But, as too often occurs, they were taking one particular fly which was on the water, and would look at nothing else.

"Oh, bother them!" cried Ricardo. "I can't find a fly in my book in the least like that little black one they are feeding on!"

He tried half-a-dozen different fly-hooks, but all to no purpose; he lost his temper, got his tackle entangled in Jaqueline's hair and then in the landing-net; and, though such a big boy, he was nearly crying with vexation.

The Princess Jaqueline, with great pains and patience, disentangled the casting line, first from her hair, which Ricardo was anxious to cut (the

Drifting before a light breeze.

great stupid oaf,—her pretty hair!) then from the landing-net; but Dick had grown sulky.

"It's no use," he said; "I have not a fly that will suit. Let's go home," and he threw a tin can at a rising trout.

"Now, Dick," said Jaqueline, "you know I can help you. I did not learn magic for nothing. Just you look the other way for a minute or two, and you will find the right fly at the end of your line."

Dick turned his head away (it is not proper to look on at magical arts), and then in a moment, saw the right hook on his cast; but Jaqueline was not in the boat. She had turned herself into an artificial fly (a small black gnat), and Dick might set to his sport again.

"What a trump that girl is," he said aloud. "Clever, too!" and he began casting. He got a trout every cast, great big ones, over a pound, and soon he had a basketful. But he began to feel rather bored.

"There's not much fun taking them," he said, "when they are so silly."

At that very moment he noticed that the fly was off his cast, and Jaqueline was sitting at the oars.

"You see, Ricardo," she said, "I was right after all. There is not much pleasure in sport that is easy and certain. Now, apply this moral to dragon-killing with magic instruments. It may be useful when one is obliged to defend oneself, but surely a prince ought not to give his whole time to nothing else!"

Dick had no answer ready, so he only grumbled:

"You're always preaching at me, Jack; everybody always is. I seem to have been born just to be preached at."

Some people are; and it does grow rather tedious in the long run. But perhaps what Jaqueline said may have made some impression on Ricardo, for he stuck to his books for weeks, and was got into decimal fractions and Euclid.

All this, of course, pleased the king very much, and he began to entertain hopes of Ricardo's becoming a wise and learned prince, and a credit to his illustrious family.

Things were not always to go smoothly, far from it; and it was poor Jaqueline who fell into trouble next. She had been very ready to lecture Dick, as we saw, and took a good deal of credit to herself for his steadiness. But one day King Prigio happened to meet Jaqueline's maid, Rosina, on the stairs; and as Rosina was a pretty girl, and the king was always kind to his dependents, he stopped to have a chat with her.

"Why, Rosina, what a pretty little silver cross you are wearing," he said, and he lifted a curious ornament which hung from a chain on Rosina's neck. It consisted of seven drops of silver, set like this:

```
      o
      o
    o o o
      o
      o
```

"May I look at it?" his Majesty asked, and Rosina, all in a flutter, took it off and gave it to him. "H'm!" said the king. "Very curious and pretty! May I ask you where you got this, Rosina?"

Now Rosina generally had her answer ready, and I am very sorry to say that she did not always speak the truth when she could think of anything better. On this occasion she was anxious to think of something better, for fear of getting Jaqueline into a scrape about the chemical experiment in her bedroom. But Rosina was fluttered, as we said, by the royal kindness, and she could think of nothing but to curtsy, and say:

"Please, your Majesty, the princess gave me the drops."

"Very interesting," said the king. "There is a little white moon shining in each of them! I wonder if they shine in the dark?"

He opened the door of a cupboard which had no windows, where the housemaid kept her mops and brooms, and shut himself in. Yes, there was

"H'm!" said the king. "Very curious and pretty!"

no mistake; the darkness was quite lighted up with the sheen of the seven little moons in the silver. The king looked rather grave.

"If you can trust me with this cross till to-morrow, Rosina, I should like to have it examined and analysed. This is no common silver."

Of course Rosina could only curtsy, but she was very much alarmed about the consequences to her mistress.

After luncheon, the king asked Jaqueline to come into his study, as he often did, to help him with his letters. When they had sat down, his Majesty said:

"My dear Jaqueline, I never interfere with your pursuits, but I almost doubt whether *Cornelius Agrippa* is a good book for a very young lady to read. The Fairy Paribanou, I am sure, taught you nothing beyond the ordinary magical accomplishments suited to your rank; but there are a great many things in the *Cornelius* which I think you should not study till you are older and wiser."

"What does your Majesty mean?" said poor Jaqueline, feeling very uncomfortable; for the king had never lectured her before.

"Why," said his Majesty, taking the silver cross out of his pocket, "did you not give this to Rosina?"

"Yes, sire, I did give her the drops. She had them made up herself."

"Then give it back to her when you see her next. I am glad you are frank, Jaqueline. And you know, of course, that the drops are not ordinary silver? They are moon silver, and that can only be got in one way, so far as I know, at least—when one spills the water when he, or she, is drinking the moon. Now, there is only one book which tells how that can be done, and there is only one reason for doing it; namely, to find out what is some other person's secret. I shall not ask you *whose* secret you wanted to find out, but I must request you never to do such a thing again without consulting me. You can have no reason for it, such as a great king might have whose enemies are plotting against his country."

"Oh, sire, I will tell you everything!" cried Jaqueline.

"No, don't; I don't want to know. I am sure you will make no use of your information which you think I should not approve of. But there is another thing — that eclipse of the moon! Oh, Jaqueline, was it honourable, or fair to the astronomers and men of science, to say nothing about it? Their European reputations are seriously injured."

Poor Jaqueline could only cry.

"Never mind," said his Majesty, comforting her. "There is no great harm done yet, and perhaps they would not believe you if you did explain; but just think, if some people ceased to believe in Science, what would they have left to believe in? But you are young, of course, and cannot be expected to think of everything."

"I never thought about it at all," wept Jaqueline.

"'Evil is wrought by want of thought,'" said the king, quoting the poet. "Now run away, dry your tears, and I think you had better bring me that book, and I'll put it back in one of the locked-up shelves. Later, when you are older, we shall see about it."

The princess flew to her room, and returned with her book. And the king kissed her, and told her to go and see if her Majesty meant to take a drive.

"I'll never deceive him again, never . . . unless it is *quite* necessary," said the princess to herself. "Indeed, it is not so easy to deceive the king. What a lot he has read!"

In fact, King Prigio had been very studious when a young man, before he came to the throne.

"Poor child!" thought the king. "No doubt she was trying her fortune, wondering if Ricardo cares for her a little. Of course I could not let her tell me *that*, poor child!"

In this guess, as we know, his Majesty was mistaken, which seldom happened to him.

"I wonder who she is?" the king went on, speaking to himself. "That great booby, Ricardo, saved her from wild birds, which were just going to eat her. She was fastened to a mountain top, but *where?* that's the question. Ricardo never has any notion of geography. It was across the sea, he noticed *that;* but which sea,—Atlantic, Pacific, the Black Sea, the Caspian, the Sea of Marmora, the Red Sea, the Indian Ocean, the German Ocean, the Mediterranean? Her ornaments were very peculiar; there was a broad gold sun on her breast. I must look at them again some day. She said she was being sacrificed to wild birds (which her people worshipped), because there was some famine, or war, or trouble in the country. She said she was a Daughter of the Sun; but that, of course, is absurd, unless—— By Jove! I believe I have it," said the king, and he went into the royal library and was looking for some old Spanish book, when his secretary came and said that the Russian Ambassador was waiting for an interview with his Majesty.

"Dismal old Muscovite!" sighed the king. "A monarch has not a moment to himself for his private studies. Ah, Prigio! why wert thou not born to a private station? But Duty before everything," and wreathing his royal countenance in smiles, his Majesty prepared to give Count Snoreonski an audience.

It was all about the attitude of Pantouflia in the event of a Polish invasion of Russia. The king reassured Count Snoreonski, affirming that Pantouflia, while deeply regretting the disturbed relations between two States in whose welfare she was deeply interested, would ever preserve an attitude of benevolent neutrality, unless her own interests were threatened.

"I may give your message to my august mistress, the Czarina?" said the ambassador.

"By all means, adding an expression of my tender interest in her Majesty's health and welfare," said the king, presenting the count at the same time with a magnificent diamond snuffbox containing his portrait.

The old count was affected to tears, and withdrew, while King Prigio said:

"I have not lost a day; I have made an amiable but very stupid man happy."

Such are, or rather such were, the toils of monarchs!

CHAPTER V.

Prince Ricardo Crosses the Path of History.

"I SAY, Jack," said Prince Ricardo one morning, "here's a queer letter for me!"

King Prigio had gone to a distant part of his dominions, on business of importance, and the young people were sitting in the royal study. The letter, which Ricardo handed to Jaqueline, was written on a great broad sheet of paper, folded up without any envelope, as was the custom then, and was sealed with a huge seal in red wax.

"I don't know the arms," Ricardo said.

"Oh, Ricardo, how you *do* neglect your Heraldry! Old Green Stocking is in despair over your ignorance."

Now Green Stocking was the chief herald of Pantouflia, just like Blue Mantle in England.

"Why, these are the Royal Arms of England, you great ignorant Dick!"

"But Rome isn't in England, is it?—and the post-mark is 'Roma': that's Rome in some lingo, I expect. It is in Latin, anyhow, I know. *Mortuus est Romæ* — 'He died at Rome.' It's in the Latin Grammar. Let's see what the fellow says, anyhow," added Ricardo, breaking the seal.

"He begins, 'Prins and dear Cousin!' I say, Jaqueline, he spells it 'Prins;' now it is P-R-I-N-C-E. He *must* be an ignorant fellow!"

"People in glass houses should not throw stones, Dick," said Jaqueline.

"He signs himself 'Charles, P. W.,'" said Ricardo, looking at the end. "Who on earth can he be? Why does he not put 'P. W. Charles,' if these are his initials? Look here, it's rather a long letter; you might read it to us, Jack!"

The princess took the epistle and began:

"How nice it smells, all scented! The paper is gilt-edged, too."

"Luxurious beggar, whoever he is," said Ricardo.

"Well, he says: 'Prins and dear Cousin,— You and me' (oh, what grammar!) 'are much the same age, I being fifteen next birthday, and we should be better *ackwainted*. All the wurld has herd of the fame of Prins Ricardo, whose name is *feerd*, and his *sord* dreded, wherever there are Monsters and Tirants. Prins, you may be less well informed about my situation. I have not killed any Dragguns, there being nun of them here; but I have been *under fiar*, at Gaeta.' Where's Gaeta, Dick?"

"Never heard of it," said Ricardo.

"Well, it is in Italy, and it was besieged lately. He goes on: 'and I am told that I did not misbehave myself, nor disgrace *the blud of Bruce.*'"

"I've heard of Robert Bruce," said Dick; "he was the man who did not kill the spider, but he cracked the head of Sir Harry Bohun with one whack of his axe. I remember *him* well enough."

"Well, your correspondent seems to be a descendant of his."

"That's getting more interesting," said Dick. "I wish my father would go to war with somebody. With the Sword of Sharpness I'd make the enemy whistle! Drive on, Jack."

"'As a prins in distress, I apeal to your valler, so renouned in Europe. I am kept out of my own; my royal father, King Gems,'— well, this is the worst spelling I ever saw in my life! He means King *James*,—'my royal father, King Gems, being druv into exile by a crewl Usurper, the Elector of Hannover. King Gems is *old*, and likes a quiat life; but I am determined to make an effort, if I go alone, and Europe shall here of Prince Charles. Having heard—as who has not?—of your royal Highness's courage and sordsmanship, I throw myself at your feet, and implore you to asist a prins in distres. Let our sords be drawn together in the caus of freedom and an outraged country, my own.

"'I remain,

"'Prins and dear Cuzen,

"'Charles, P. W.'

"P. W. means Prince of Wales," added Jaqueline. "He is turned out of England, you know, and lives at Rome with his father."

"I like that chap," said Prince Ricardo. "He does not spell very well, as you say, but I sometimes make mistakes myself; and I like his spirit. I've been looking out for an adventure; but the big game is getting shy, and my sword rusts in his scabbard. I'll tell you what, Jack—I've an idea! I'll put him on the throne of his fathers; it's as easy as shelling peas: and as for that other fellow, the Elector, I'll send him back to Hanover, wherever that may be, and he can go on electing, and polling his vote in peace and quietness, at home. Just wait till I spot the places."

The prince ran up to the turret, fetched the magic spy-glass, and looked up London, Rome, and Hanover, as you would in a map.

"Well, Dick, but how do you mean to do it?"

"Do it?—nothing simpler! I just take my Seven-league Boots, run over to Rome, pick up Prince Charles, put him on the magic carpet, fly to London, clap the Cap of Darkness on him so that nobody can see him, set him down on the throne of his fathers; pick up the Elector, carry him over to his beloved Hanover, and the trick is done—what they call a bloodless revolution in the history books."

"But if the English don't like Prince Charles when they get him?"

"Like him? they're sure to like him, a young fellow like that! Besides, I'll take the sword with me in case of accidents."

"But, Dick, it is your father's rule that you are never to meddle in the affairs of other countries, and never to start on an expedition when he is not at home."

"Oh, he won't mind this time! There's no kind of danger; and I'm sure he will approve of the *principle* of the thing. Kings must stick up for each other. Why, some electing characters might come here and kick *us* out!"

"Your father is not the sort of king who is kicked out," said Jaqueline.

But there was no use in talking to Dick. He made his simple preparations, and announced that he would be back in time for luncheon.

What was poor Jaqueline to do?

She was extremely anxious. She knew, as we saw, what King Prigio had intended about changing the fairy things for others that would not work. She was certain Dick would get himself into a scrape; how was she to help him? She made up her mind quickly, while Dick was putting his things together. She told the queen (it was the nearest to the truth she could think of) that she "was going for a turn with Dick." Then she changed herself into a mosquito—a kind of gnat that bites—and hid herself under a fold of Dick's coat. Of course he knew nothing about her being there. Then he started off in his Seven-league Boots, and before you could say "Jack Robinson" he was in Rome, in the grounds of a splendid palace called the Villa Borghese.

There he saw an elderly gentleman, in a great curled wig, sound asleep on a seat beneath a tree. The old gentleman had a long, pale, melancholy face, and across his breast was a broad blue ribbon with a star. Ah! how changed was King James from the handsome Prince who had loved fair Beatrix Esmond, thirty years ago! Near him were two boys, not quite so old as Prince Ricardo. The younger was a pretty dark boy, with a funny little roundabout white wig. He was splendidly dressed in a light-blue silk coat; a delicate little lace scarf was tied round his neck; he had lace ruffles falling about his little ringed hands; he had a pretty sword, with a gold handle set with diamonds—in fact, he was the picture of a little dandy. The other lad had a broad Scotch bonnet on, and no wig; beautiful silky yellow locks fell about his shoulders. He had laid his sword on the grass. He was dressed in tartan, which Ricardo had never seen before; and he wore a kilt, which was also new to Ricardo, who wondered at his bare legs—for he was wearing shoes with no stockings. In his hand he held a curious club, with a long, slim handle, and a head made heavy with lead, and defended with horn. With this he was aiming at a little white ball; and suddenly he swung up the club and sent the ball out of sight in the air, over several trees.

Prince Ricardo stepped up to this boy, took off his cap, and said:

"I think I have the honour of addressing the Prince of Wales?"

Prince Charles started at the sight of a gentleman in long riding-boots, girt with a broadsword, which was not then generally worn, and carrying a Persian rug under his arm.

"That is what I am called, sir," he said, "by those who give me the title which is mine by right. May I inquire the reason which offers me the pleasure of this unexpected interview?"

"Oh, I'm Ricardo of Pantouflia!" says Dick. "I had a letter from you this morning, and I believe you wanted to see me."

"From Pantouflia, sir," said Prince Charles; "why, that is hundreds of leagues away!"

"It is a good distance," said Dick; "but a mere step when you wear Seven-league Boots, like mine."

"My dear prince," said Charles, throwing himself into his arms with rapture, and kissing him in the Italian fashion, which Dick did not half like, "you are, indeed, worthy of your reputation; and these are the celebrated Seven-league Boots? Harry," he cried to his brother, "come here at once and let me present you to his Royal Highness, our illustrious ally, Prince Ricardo of Pantouflia. The Duke of York— Prince Ricardo of Pantouflia. Gentlemen, know each other!"

The prince bowed in the most stately manner.

"I say," said Dick, who was seldom at all up to the standard of royal conversation, "what's that game you were playing? It's new to me. You sent the ball a tremendous long shot."

"The game is called golf, and is the favourite pastime of my loyal Scottish subjects," said Prince Charles. "For that reason, that I may be able to share the amusements of my people, whom I soon hope to lead to a glorious victory, followed by a peaceful and prosperous reign, I am acquiring a difficult art. I'm practising walking without stockings, too, to harden my feet," he said, in a more familiar tone of voice. "I fancy there are plenty of long marches before me, and I would not be a spear's length behind the hardiest Highlander."

"By Jove! I respect you," said Dick, with the greatest sincerity; "but I don't think, with me on your side, you will need to make many marches. It will all be plain sailing."

"Pray explain your plan," said Prince Charles. "The task of conquering back the throne of my fathers is not so simple as you seem to suppose."

"I've done a good many difficult things," said Dick, modestly.

"The conqueror of the magician, Gorgonzola, and the Giant Who never Knew when he had Enough, need not tell me that," said Prince Charles, with a courteous allusion to two of Ricardo's most prodigious adventures.

"Oh! I've very little to be proud of, really," said Dick, blushing; "anyone could do as much with my fairy things, of which, no doubt, you have heard. With a Sword of Sharpness and a Cap of Darkness, and so forth, you have a great pull over almost anything."

"And you really possess those talismans?" said the prince.

"Certainly I do. You see how short a time I took in coming to your call from Pantouflia."

"And has Holy Church," asked the Duke of York, with anxiety, "given her sanction and her blessing to those instruments of an art, usually, in her wisdom, forbidden?"

"Oh, never mind Holy Church, Harry!" said Prince Charles. "This is *business*. Besides, the English are Protestants."

"I pray for their conversion daily," said the Duke of York.

"The end justifies the means, you know," answered Prince Charles. "All's fair in love and war."

"I should think so," said Ricardo, "especially against those brutes of Electors; they give trouble at home sometimes."

"You, too, are plagued with an Elector?" asked Prince Charles.

"*An* Elector? thousands of them!" answered Dick, who never could understand anything about politics.

Prince Charles looked puzzled, but requested Dick to explain his great plan.

They sat down on the grass, and Ricardo showed them how he meant to manage it, just as he had told Jaqueline. As he said, nothing could be simpler.

"Let's start at once," he said, and, inducing Prince Charles to sit down on the magic carpet, he cried:

"England! St. James's Palace!"

But nothing happened!

The carpet was not the right magic carpet, but the one which King Prigio had put in its place.

"Get on! England, I said!" cried Dick.

But there they remained, under the chestnut tree, sitting on the carpet above the flowery grass.

Prince Charles leaped to his feet; his face like fire, his eyes glowing.

"Enough of this fooling, sir!" he said. "It is easy, but cowardly, to mock at an unfortunate prince. Take your carpet and be off with you, out of the gardens, or your shoulders shall taste my club."

"There has been some mistake," Ricardo said; "the wrong carpet has been brought by accident, or the carpet has lost its power."

"In this sacred city, blessed by the presence of his Holiness the Pope, and the relics of so many martyrs and saints, magic may well cease to be potent," said the Duke of York.

"Nonsense! You are an impostor, sir! Leave my presence!" cried Prince Charles, lifting his golf-club.

Dick caught it out of his hand, and broke across his knee as fine a driver as ever came from Robertson's shop at St. Andrew's.

But there they remained.

"The quarrels of princes are not settled with clubs, sir! Draw and defend yourself!" he said, kicking off his boots and standing in his socks on the grass.

Think of the horror of poor Jaqueline, who witnessed this terrible scene of passion from a fold in Prince Ricardo's dress! What could the girl do to save the life of two princes, the hopes of one nation, and of a respectable minority in another?

In a moment Prince Charles's rapier was shining in the sunlight, and he fell on guard in the most elegant attitude, his left hand gracefully raised and curved.

Dick drew his sword, but, as suddenly, threw it down again.

"Hang it!" he exclaimed, "I can't hit you with *this!* This is the Sword of Sharpness; it would cut through your steel and your neck at a touch."

He paused, and thought.

"Let me beseech your Royal Highness," he said to the Duke of York, who was in a terrible taking, "to lend your blade to a hand not less royal than your own."

"Give him it, Hal!" said Prince Charles, who was standing with the point of his sword on the ground, and the blade bent. "He seems to believe in his own nonsense."

The duke yielded his sword; Dick took it, made a flourish, and rushed at Prince Charles.

Now Ricardo had always neglected his fencing lessons. "Where's the good of it," he used to ask, "all that stamping, and posture-making, and ha-haing? The Sword of Sharpness is enough for *me*."

But now he could not, in honour, use the Sword of Sharpness; so on he came, waving the rapier like a claymore, and made a slice at Prince Charles's head.

The prince, very much surprised, parried in prime, riposted, and touched Dick on the hand.

At this moment the Princess Jaqueline did what she should have thought of sooner. She flew out of Dick's coat, and stung old King James on his royal nose. The king wakened, nearly crushed the princess (so dangerous is the practice of magic to the artist), and then leaped up, and saw Dick's blade flying through the air, glittering in the sun. The prince had disarmed him.

"Hullo! what's all this? *À moi, mes gardes!*" cried the old king, in French and English; and then he ran up, just in time to hear Prince Charles say:

"Sir, take your life! I cannot strike an unarmed man. A prince you may be, but you have not learned the exercises of gentlemen."

"What is all this, Carluccio?" asked the old king. "Swords out! brawling in my very presence! blood drawn!" for Dick's hand was bleeding a good deal.

Prince Charles, as briefly as possible, explained the unusual nature of the circumstances.

"A king must hear both sides," said King James. "What reply have you, sir, to make to his Royal Highness's statements?"

"The carpet would not work, sir," said Dick. "It never happened before. Had I used my own sword," and he explained its properties, "the Prince of Wales would not be alive to tell his story. I can say no more, beyond offering my apology for a disappointment which I could not have foreseen. A gentleman can only say that he is sorry. But wait!" he added; "I can at least prove that my confidence in some of my resources is not misplaced. Bid me bring you something—anything—from the ends of the earth, and it shall be in your hands. I can't say fairer."

King James reflected, while Prince Ricardo was pulling on the Seven-league Boots, which he had kicked off to fight more freely, and while the Duke of York bandaged Dick's hand with a kerchief.

"Bring me," said his Majesty, "Lord Lovat's snuff-mull."

"Where does he live?" said Dick.

"At Gortuleg, in Scotland," answered King James.

Dick was out of sight before the words were fairly spoken, and in ten minutes was back, bearing a large ram's-horn snuff-box, with a big cairngorm set in the top, and the Frazer arms.

"Most astonishing!" said King James.

"A miracle!" said the Duke of York.

"You have entirely cleared your character," said the king. "Your honour is without a stain, though it is a pity about the carpet. Your nobility in not using your magical sword, under the greatest provocation, reconciles me to this fresh blighting of my hopes. All my allies fail me," said the poor king with a sigh; "you alone have failed with honour. Carluccio, embrace the prince!"

They fell into each other's arms.

"Prince," said Dick, "you have taught me a lesson for which I shall not be ungrateful. With any blade a gentleman should be able to hold his own in fair fight. I shall no longer neglect my fencing lessons."

"With any blade," said Prince Charles, "I shall be happy to find Prince Ricardo by my side in a stricken field. We shall not part till I have induced you to accept a sword which I can never hope to draw against another adversary so noble. In war, my weapon is the claymore."

Here the prince offered to Ricardo the ruby-studded hilt of his rapier, which had a beautiful white shark-skin sheath.

"You must accept it, sir," said King James; "the hilt holds the rubies of John Sobieski."

"Thank you, prince," said Ricardo, "for the weapon, which I shall learn to wield; and I entreat you to honour me by receiving this fairy gift — which *you* do not need — a ring which makes all men faithful to the wearer."

The Prince of Wales bowed, and placed the talisman on his finger.

Ricardo then, after a few words of courtesy on both parts, picked up his useless carpet, took his farewell of the royal party, and, with Jaqueline still hidden under his collar, returned at full speed, but with a heavy heart, to Pantouflia, where the palace gong was just sounding for luncheon.

Ricardo never interfered in foreign affairs again, but his ring proved very useful to Prince Charles, as you may have read in history.

CHAPTER VI.

Ricardo's Repentance.

THE queen, as it happened fortunately, was lunching with one of the ladies of her Court. Ricardo did not come down to luncheon, and Jaqueline ate hers alone; and very mournful she felt. The prince had certainly not come well out of the adventure. He had failed (as all attempts to restore the Stuarts always did); he had been wounded, though he had never received a scratch in any of his earlier exploits; and if his honour was safe, and his good intentions fully understood, that was chiefly due to Jaqueline, and to the generosity of King James and Prince Charles.

"I wonder what he's doing?" she said to

herself, and at last she went up and knocked at Ricardo's door.

"Go away," he said; "I don't want to see anybody. Who is it?"

"It's only me—Jaqueline."

"Go away! I want nobody."

"Do let me in, dear Dick; I have good news for you," said the princess.

"What is it?" said Ricardo, unlocking the door. "Why do you bother a fellow so?"

He had been crying—his hand obviously hurt him badly; he looked, and indeed he was, very sulky.

"How did you get on in England, Dick?" asked the princess, taking no notice of his bandaged hand.

"Oh, don't ask me!" said Ricardo. "I've not been to England at all."

"Why, what happened?"

"Everything that is horrid happened," said Dick; and then, unable to keep it any longer to himself, he said: "I've failed to keep my promise; I've been insulted, I've been beaten by a fellow younger than myself; and, oh! how my hand does hurt, and I've got such a headache! And what am I to say to my mother when she asks why my arm is in a sling? and what will my father say? I'm quite broken down and desperate. I think I'll run away to sea;" and indeed he looked very wild and miserable.

"*It's only me.*"

"Tell me how it all happened, Dick," said the princess; "I'm sure it's not so bad as you make out. Perhaps I can help you."

"How can a girl help a man?" cried Dick, angrily; and poor Jaqueline, remembering how she *had* helped him, at the risk of her own life, when King James nearly crushed her in the shape of a mosquito, turned her head away, and cried silently.

"I'm a beast," said Dick. "I beg your pardon, Jack dear. You are always a trump, I will say; but I don't see what you can do."

Then he told her all the story (which, of course, she knew perfectly well already), except the part played by the mosquito, of which he could not be aware.

"I was sure it was not so bad as you made it out, Dick," she said. "You see, the old king, who is not very wise, but is a perfectly honourable gentleman, gave you the highest praise."

She thought of lecturing him a little about disobeying his father, but it did not seem a good opportunity. Besides, Jaqueline had been lectured herself lately, and had not enjoyed it.

"What am I to say to my mother?" Dick repeated.

"We must think of something to say," said Jaqueline.

"I can't tell my mother anything but the

truth," Ricardo went on. "Here's my hand, how it does sting! and she must find out."

"I think I can cure it," said Jaqueline. "Didn't you say Prince Charles gave you his own sword?"

"Yes, there it is; but what has that to do with it?"

"Everything in the world to do with it, my dear Dick. How lucky it is that he gave it to you!"

And she ran to her own room, and brought a beautiful golden casket, which contained her medicines.

Taking out a small phial, marked (in letters of emerald):

"Weapon Salve,"

the princess drew the bright sword, extracted a little of the ointment from the phial, and spread it on a soft silk handkerchief.

"What are you going to do with the sword?" asked Ricardo.

"Polish it a little," said Jaqueline, smiling, and she began gently to rub, with the salve, the point of the rapier.

As she did so, Ricardo's arm ceased to hurt, and the look of pain passed from his mouth.

"Why, I feel quite better!" he said. "I can use my hand as well as ever."

Then he took off the stained handkerchief, and, lo, there was not even a mark where the wound had been! For this was the famous Weapon Salve which you may read about in Sir Kenelm Digby, and which the Lady of Branxholme used, in *The Lay of the Last Minstrel*. But the secret of making it has long been lost, except in Pantouflia.

"You are the best girl in the world, Jaqueline," said Ricardo. "You may give me a kiss if you like; and I won't call you 'Jack,' or laugh at you for reading books, any more. There's something in books after all."

The princess did not take advantage of Dick's permission, but advised him to lie down and try to sleep.

"I say, though," he said, "what about my father?"

"The king need never be told anything about it," said Jaqueline, "need he?"

"Oh, that won't do! I tell my father everything; but then, I never had anything like this to tell him before. Don't you think, Jaqueline, you might break it to him? He's very fond of you. Just tell him what I told you; it's every word of it true, and he ought to know. He might see something about it in the *Mercure de France*."

This was the newspaper of the period.

"I don't think it will get into the papers," said Jaqueline, smiling. "Nobody could tell, except the king and the princes, and they have reasons for keeping it to themselves."

"I don't trust that younger one," said Dick, moodily; "I don't care for that young man. Anyway, my father *must* be told; and, if you won't, I must."

"Well, I'll tell him," said Jaqueline. "And now lie down till evening."

After dinner, in the conservatory, Jaqueline told King Prigio all about it.

His Majesty was very much moved.

"What extraordinary bad luck that family has!" he thought. "If I had not changed the rug, the merest accident, Prince Charles would have dined at St. James's to-night, and King George in Hanover. It was the very nearest thing!"

"This meddling with practical affairs will never do," he said aloud.

"Dick has had a lesson, sire," said the princess. "He says he'll never mix himself up with politics again, whatever happens. And he says he means to study all about them, for he feels frightfully ignorant, and, above all, he means to practise his fencing."

These remarks were not part of the conversation between Ricardo and Jaqueline, but she considered that Dick *meant* all this, and, really, he did.

"That is well, as far as it goes," said the king. "But, Jaqueline, about that mosquito?" for she had told him this part of the adventure. "That was a very convenient mosquito, though

I don't know how Dick was able to observe it from any distance. I see *your* hand in that, my dear, and I am glad you can make such kind and wise use of the lessons of the good Fairy Paribanou. Jaqueline," he added solemnly, laying his hand on her head, " you have saved the honour of Pantouflia, which is dearer to me than life. Without your help, I tremble to think what might have occurred."

The princess blushed very much, and felt very happy.

" Now run away to the queen, my dear," said his Majesty, " I want to think things over."

He did think them over, and the more he thought the more he felt the inconvenience attending the possession of fairy things.

"An eclipse one day, as nearly as possible a revolution soon after !" he said to himself. "But for Jaqueline, Ricardo's conduct would have been blazed abroad, England would have been irritated. It is true she cannot get at Pantouflia very easily; we have no sea-coast, and we are surrounded by friendly countries. But it would have been a ticklish and discreditable position. I must really speak to Dick," which he did next morning after breakfast.

" You have broken my rules, Ricardo," he said. " True, there is no great harm done, and you have confessed frankly; but how am I to trust you any longer ? "

" I'll give you my sacred word of honour,

father, that I'll never meddle with politics again, or start on an expedition, without telling you. I have had enough of it. And I'll turn over a new leaf. I've learned to be ashamed of my ignorance; and I've sent for Francalanza, and I'll fence every day, and read like anything."

"Very good," said the king. "I believe you mean what you say. Now go to your fencing lesson."

"But, I say, father," cried Ricardo, "was it not strange about the magic carpet?"

"I told you not to trust to these things," said the king. "Some enchanter may have deprived it of its power, it may be worn out, someone may have substituted a common Persian rug; anything may happen. You *must* learn to depend on yourself. Now, be off with you, I'm busy. And remember, you don't stir without my permission."

The prince ran off, and presently the sounds of stamping feet and "*un, deux; doublez, dégagez, vite; contre de carte,*" and so forth, might be heard over a great part of the royal establishment.

CHAPTER VII.

Prince Ricardo and an Old Enemy.

"THERE is one brute I wish I could get upsides with," said Ricardo, at breakfast one morning, his mouth full of sardine.

"Really, Ricardo, your language is most unprincely," said his august father; "I am always noticing it. You mean, I suppose, that there is one enemy of the human race whom you wish to abolish. What is the name of the doomed foe?"

"Well, he is the greatest villain in history," said Ricardo. "You must have read about him, sir, the Yellow Dwarf."

"Yes, I have certainly studied what is told

us about him," said the king. "He is no favourite of mine."

"He is the only one, if you notice, sir, of all the scoundrels about whom our ancestors inform us, who escaped the doom which he richly merited at the sword of a good knight."

You may here remark that, since Dick took to his studies, he could speak, when he chose, like a printed book, which was by no means the case before.

"If you remember, sir, he polished off—I mean, he slew—the King of the Golden Mines and the beautiful, though frivolous, Princess Frutilla. All that the friendly Mermaid could do for them was to turn them into a pair of beautiful trees which intertwine their branches. Not much use in *that*, sir! And nothing was done to the scoundrel. He may be going on still; and, with your leave, I'll go and try a sword-thrust with him. Francalanza says I'm improving uncommon."

"You'll take the usual Sword of Sharpness," said his Majesty.

"What, sir, to a dwarf? Not I, indeed: a common small sword is good enough to settle *him*."

"They say he is very cunning of fence," said the king; "and besides, I have heard something of a diamond sword that he stole from the King of the Golden Mines."

"Very likely he has lost it or sold it, the

shabby little miscreant; however, I'll risk it. And now I must make my preparations."

The king did not ask what they were; as a rule, they were simple. But, being in the shop of the optician that day, standing with his back to the door, he heard Dick come in and order a pair of rose-coloured spectacles, with which he was at once provided. The people of Pantouflia were accustomed to wear them, saying that they improved the complexions of ladies whom they met, and added cheerfulness to things in general.

"Just plain rose-coloured glass, Herr Spex," said Dick, "I'm not short-sighted."

"The boy is beginning to show some sense," said the king to himself, knowing the nature and the difficulties of the expedition.

Ricardo did not disguise his intention of taking with him a Dandie Dinmont terrier, named Pepper, and the king, who understood the motive of this precaution, silently approved.

"The lad has come to some purpose and forethought," the king said, and he gladly advanced a considerable sum for the purchase of crocodiles' eggs, which can rarely be got quite fresh. When Jaqueline had made the crocodiles' eggs, with millet-seed and sugar-candy, into a cake for the Dwarf's lions, Ricardo announced that his preparations were complete.

Not to be the mere slave of custom, he made

Yellow. He knew that this showed the neighbourhood of Jaunia, or Daunia, the country of the Yellow Dwarf. He therefore drew bridle, placed his rose-coloured spectacles on his nose, and put spurs to his horse, for the yellow light of Jaunia makes people melancholy and cowardly. As he pricked on, his horse stumbled and nearly came on its nose. The prince noticed that a steel chain had been drawn across the road.

"What caitiff has dared!" he exclaimed, when his hat was knocked off by a well-aimed orange from a neighbouring orange-tree, and a vulgar voice squeaked:

"Hi, Blinkers!"

There was the Yellow Dwarf, an odious little figure, sitting sucking an orange in the tree, swinging his wooden shoes, and grinning all over his wrinkled face.

"Well, young Blinkers!" said the Dwarf, "what are you doing on my grounds? You're a prince, by your look. Yah! down with kings! I'm a man of the people!"

"You're a dwarf of the worst description, that's what *you* are," said Ricardo; "and let me catch you, and I'll flog the life out of you with my riding-whip!"

The very face of the Dwarf, even seen through rose-coloured spectacles, made him nearly ill.

"Yes, when you can catch me," said the Dwarf;

"but that's not to-day, nor yet to-morrow. What are you doing here? Are you an ambassador, maybe come to propose a match for me? I'm not proud, I'll hear you. They say there's a rather well-looking wench in your parts, the Princess Jaqueline——"

"Mention that lady's name, you villain," cried Dick, "and I'll cut down your orange-tree!" and he wished he had brought the Sword of Sharpness, for you cannot prod down a tree with the point of a rapier.

"Fancy her yourself?" said the Dwarf, showing his yellow teeth with a detestable grin; while Ricardo turned quite white with anger, and not knowing how to deal with this insufferable little monster.

"I'm a widower, I am," said the Dwarf, "though I'm out of mourning," for he wore a dirty clay-coloured Yellow jacket. "My illustrious consort, the Princess Frutilla, did not behave very nice, and I had to avenge my honour; in fact, I'm open to any offers, however humble. Going at an alarming sacrifice! Come to my box" (and he pointed to a filthy clay cottage, all surrounded by thistles, nettles, and black boggy water), "and I'll talk over your proposals."

"Hold your impudent tongue!" said Dick. "The Princess Frutilla was an injured saint; and as for the lady whom I shall not name in your polluting presence,

I am her knight, and I defy you to deadly combat!"

We may imagine how glad the princess was when (disguised as a wasp) she heard Dick say he was her knight; not that, in fact, he had thought of it before.

"Oh! you're for a fight, are you?" sneered the Dwarf. "I might tell you to hit one of your own weight, but I'm not afraid of six of you. Yah! mammy's brat! Look here, young Blinkers, I don't want to hurt you. Just turn old Dobbin's head, and trot back to your mammy, Queen Rosalind, at Pantouflia. Does she know you're out?"

"I'll be into *you*, pretty quick," said Ricardo. "But why do I bandy words with a miserable peasant?"

"And don't get much the best of them either," said the Dwarf, provokingly. "But I'll fight, if you will have it."

The prince leaped from his horse, leaving Pepper on the saddle-bow.

No sooner had he touched the ground than the Dwarf shouted:

"Hi! to him, Billy! to him, Daniel! at him, good lions, at him!" and, with an awful roar, two lions rushed from a neighbouring potato-patch and made for Ricardo. These were not ordinary lions, history avers, each having two heads, each being eight feet high, with four rows of teeth; their skins as hard as nails, and bright red, like morocco.*

The prince did not lose his presence of mind; hastily he threw the cake of crocodiles' eggs, millet-seed, and sugar-candy to the lions. This is a dainty which lions can never resist, and running greedily at it, with four tremendous snaps, they got hold of each other by their jaws, and their eight rows of teeth were locked fast in a grim and deadly *struggle for existence!*

The Dwarf took in the affair at a glance.

"Cursed be he who taught you this!" he cried, and then whistled in a shrill and vulgar manner on his very dirty fingers. At his call rushed up an enormous Spanish cat, ready saddled and bridled, and darting fire from its eyes. To leap on its back, while Ricardo sprang on his own steed, was to the active Dwarf the work of a moment. Then clapping spurs to its sides (his spurs grew naturally on his bare heels, horrible to relate, like a cock's spurs) and taking his cat by the head, the Dwarf forced it to leap on to Ricardo's saddle. The diamond sword which slew the king of the Golden Mines —that invincible sword which hews iron like a reed—was up and flashing in the air!

At this very moment King Prigio, seeing, in the magic globe, all that passed, and despairing of Ricardo's life, was just about to wish the

* See the works of D'Aulnoy.

dwarf at Jericho, when through the open window, with a tremendous whirr, came a huge vulture, and knocked the king's wishing cap off! Wishing was now of no use.

This odious fowl was the Fairy of the Desert, the Dwarf's trusted ally in every sort of mischief. The vulture flew instantly out of the window; and ah! with what awful anxiety the king again turned his eyes on the crystal ball only a parent's heart can know. Should he see Ricardo bleeding at the feet of the abominable dwarf? The king scarcely dared to look; never before had he known the nature of fear. However, look he did, and saw the dwarf uncatted, and Pepper, the gallant Dandie Dinmont, with his teeth in the throat of the monstrous Spanish cat.

No sooner had he seen the cat leap on his master's saddle-bow than Pepper, true to the instinct of his race, sprang at its neck, just behind the head—the usual place,—and, with an awful and despairing mew, the cat (Peter was its name) gave up its life.

The dwarf was on his feet in a moment, waving the diamond sword, which lighted up the whole scene, and yelling taunts. Pepper was flying at his heels, and, with great agility, was keeping out of the way of the invincible blade.

"Ah!" screamed the Dwarf as Pepper got him by the ankle. "Call off your dog, you coward, and come down off your horse, and fight fair!"

At this moment, *bleeding yellow blood*, dusty, mad with pain, the dwarf was a sight to strike terror into the boldest.

Dick sprang from his saddle, but so terrific was the appearance of his adversary, and so dazzling was the sheen of the diamond sword, that he put his hand in his pocket, drew out, as he supposed, the sham Cap of Darkness, and placed it on his head.

"Yah! who's your hatter?" screamed the infuriated dwarf. "*I* see you!" and he disengaged, feinted in carte, and made a lunge in seconde at Dick which no mortal blade could have parried. The prince (thanks to his excellent training) just succeeded in stepping aside, but the dwarf recovered with astonishing quickness.

"Coward, *lâche*, poltroon, runaway!" he hissed through his clenched teeth, and was about to make a thrust in tierce which must infallibly have been fatal, when the Princess Jaqueline, in her shape as a wasp, stung him fiercely on the wrist.

With an oath so awful that we dare not set it down, the dwarf dropped the diamond sword, sucked his injured limb, and began hopping about with pain.

In a moment Prince Ricardo's foot was on the blade of the diamond sword, which he

The fight with the Yellow Dwarf.

passed thrice through the body of the Yellow Dwarf. Squirming fearfully, the little monster expired, his last look a defiance, his latest word an insult:

"Yah! Gig-lamps!"

Prince Ricardo wiped the diamond blade clean from its yellow stains.

"Princess Frutilla is avenged!" he cried. Then pensively looking at his fallen foe, "Peace to his ashes," he said; "he died in harness!"

Turning at the word, he observed that the two lions were stiff and dead, locked in each other's gory jaws!

At that moment King Prigio, looking in the crystal ball, gave a great sigh of relief.

"All's well that ends well," he said, lighting a fresh cigar, for he had allowed the other to go out in his excitement, "but it was a fight! I am not satisfied," his Majesty went on reflecting, "with this plan of changing the magical articles. The first time was of no great importance, and I could not know that the boy would start on an expedition without giving me warning. But, in to-day's affair he owes his safety entirely to himself and Pepper," for he had not seen the wasp. "The Fairy of the Desert quite baffled me: it was terrible. I shall restore the right fairy things to-night. As to the Fairy of the Desert," he said, forgetting that his Wishing Cap was on, "I wish she were dead!"

A hollow groan and the sound of a heavy body falling interrupted the king. He looked all about the room, but saw nothing. He was alone!

"She must have been in the room, invisible," said the king; and, of course, she has died in that condition. "But I must find her body!"

The king groped about everywhere, like a blind man, and at last discovered the dead body of the wicked fairy lying on the sofa. He could not see it, of course, but he felt it with his hands.

"This is very awkward," he remarked. "I cannot ring for the servants and make them take her away. There is only one plan."

So he wished she were in her family pyramid, in the Egyptian desert, and in a second the sofa was unoccupied.

"A very dangerous and revengeful enemy is now removed from Ricardo's path in life," said his Majesty, and went to dress for dinner.

Meanwhile Ricardo was riding gaily home. The yellow light of Jaunia had vanished, and pure blue sky broke overhead as soon as the dauntless Dwarf had drawn his latest breath. The poor, trembling people of the country came out of their huts and accompanied Dick, cheering, and throwing roses which had been yellow roses, but blushed red as soon as the Dwarf expired. They attended him to the frontiers of Pantouflia, singing his praises, which Ricardo had the new and inestimable pleasure of knowing to be deserved.

"It was sharp work," he said to himself, "but much more exciting and glorious than the usual business."

On his return Dick did not fail to mention the wasp, and again the king felt how great was his debt to Jaqueline. But they did not think it well to trouble the good queen with the dangers Dick had encountered.

CHAPTER VIII.

*The Giant who does not Know when he has bad Enough.**

ONE morning the post brought a truly enormous letter for Dick. It was as broad as a tablecloth, and the address was written in letters as long as a hoop-stick.

"I seem to know that hand," said Ricardo; "but I thought the fingers which held the pen had long been cold in death."

He opened, with his sword, the enormous letter, which was couched in the following terms:

"The Giant as does not know when he has had *enuf*, presents his compliments to Prince Ricardo; and I, having recovered from the effects of our little recent *rally*, will be happy to meet you in the old place for a return-match. I not

* This Giant is mentioned, and his picture is drawn, in an old manuscript of about 1875.

being handy with the pen, the Giant hopes you will excuse mistakes and bad writing."

Dick simply gazed with amazement.

"If ever I thought an enemy was killed and done for, it was that Giant," said he. "Why, I made mere mince-collops of him!"

However, he could not refuse a challenge, not to speak of his duty to rid the world of so greedy and odious a tyrant. Dick, therefore, took the usual things (which the king had secretly restored), but first he tried them—putting on the Cap of Darkness before the glass, in which he could not see himself. On second thoughts, he considered it unfair to take the cap. All the other articles were in working order. Jaqueline on this occasion followed him in the disguise of a crow, flying overhead.

On reaching the cavern—a huge tunnel in the rock—where the Giant lived, Ricardo blew a blast on the horn which hung outside, and, in obedience to a written notice, knocked also with a mace provided by the Giant for that purpose. Presently he heard heavy footsteps sounding along the cavern, and the Giant came out. He was above the common height for giants, and his whole face and body were seamed over with little red lines, crossing each other like tartan. These were marks of encounters, in which he had been cut to bits and come together again; for this was his peculiarity, which made him so dangerous. If you cut off his head, he went on just as before, only without it; and so about everything else. By dint of magic, he could put his head on again, just as if it had been his hat, if you gave him time enough. On the last occasion of their meeting, Ricardo had left him in a painfully scattered condition, and thought he was done for. But now, except that a bird had flown away with the little finger of his left hand and one of his ears, the Giant was as comfortable as anyone could be in his situation.

"Mornin' sir," he said to Dick, touching his forehead with his hand. "Glad to see you looking so well. No bad feeling, I hope, on either side?"

"None on mine, certainly," said Ricardo, holding out his hand, which the Giant took and shook; "but Duty is Duty, and giants must go. The modern world has no room for them."

"That's hearty," said the Giant; "I like a fellow of your kind. Now, shall we toss for corners?"

"All right!" said Dick, calling "Heads," and winning. He took the corner with the sun on his back and in the Giant's face. To it they went, the Giant aiming a blow with his club that would have felled an elephant.

Dick dodged, and cut off the Giant's feet at the ankles.

"First blood for the prince!" said the Giant, coming up smiling. "Half-minute time!"

He occupied the half-minute in placing the feet neatly beside each other, as if they had been a pair of boots.

Round II.—The Giant sparring for wind, Ricardo cuts him in two at the waist.

The Giant folded his legs up neatly, like a pair of trousers, and laid them down on a rock. He had now some difficulty in getting rapidly over the ground, and stood mainly on the defensive, and on his waist.

Round III.—Dick bisects the Giant. Both sides now attack him on either hand, and the feet kick him severely.

"No kicking!" said Dick.

"Nonsense; all fair in war!" said the Giant.

But do not let us pursue this sanguinary encounter in all its *horrible details*.

Let us also remember—otherwise the scene would be too painful for an elegant mind to contemplate with entertainment—that the Giant was in excellent training, and thought no more of a few wounds than you do of a crack on the leg from a cricket-ball. He well deserved the title given him by the Fancy, of "The Giant who does not Know when he has had Enough."

* * * *

The contest was over; Dick was resting on a rock. The lists were strewn with interesting but imperfect fragments of the Giant, when a set of double teeth of enormous size flew up out of the ground and caught Ricardo by the throat! In vain he strove to separate the teeth, when the crow, stooping from the heavens, became the Princess Jaqueline, and changed Dick into a wren—a tiny bird, so small that he easily flew out of the jaws of the Giant and winged his way to a tree, whence he watched the scene.

But the poor Princess Jaqueline!

To perform the feat of changing Dick into a bird she had, of course, according to all the laws of magic, to resume her own natural form!

There she stood, a beautiful, trembling maiden, her hands crossed on her bosom, entirely at the mercy of the Giant!

No sooner had Dick escaped than the monster began to *collect himself;* and before Jaqueline could muster strength to run away or summon to her aid the lessons of the Fairy Paribanou, the Giant who never Knew when he had Enough was himself again. A boy might have climbed up a tree (for giants are no tree-climbers, any more than the grizzly bear), but Jaqueline could not climb. She merely stood, pale and trembling. She had saved Dick, but at an enormous sacrifice, for the sword and the Seven-league Boots were lying on the trampled grass. He had not brought the Cap of Darkness, and, in the shape of a wren, of course he could not carry away the other articles. Dick was rescued, that was all, and the Princess Jaqueline had sacrificed herself to her love for him.

The Giant picked himself up and pulled himself together, as we said, and then approached Jaqueline in a very civil way, for a person of his breeding, head in hand.

"Let me introduce myself," he said, and mentioned his name and titles. "May I ask what *you* are doing here, and how you came?"

Poor Jaqueline threw herself at his feet, and murmured a short and not very intelligible account of herself.

"I don't understand," said the Giant, replacing his head on his shoulders. "What to do with you, I'm sure I don't know. '*Please don't eat me*,' did you say? Why, what do you take me for? I'm not in that line at all; low, *I* call it!"

Jaqueline was somewhat comforted at these words, dropped out of the Giant's lips from a considerable height.

"But they call you 'The Giant who does not Know when he has had Enough,'" said Jaqueline.

"And proud of the title: not enough of fighting. Of *punishment* I am a glutton, or so my friends are pleased to say. A brace of oxen, a drove of sheep or two, are enough for me," the Giant went on complacently, but forgetting

"Let me introduce myself," he said.

to mention that the sheep and the oxen were the property of other people. "Where am I' to put you till your friends come and pay your ransom?" the Giant asked again, and stared at Jaqueline in a perplexed way. "I can't take you home with me, that is out of the question. I have a little woman of my own, and she's not very fond of other ladies; especially, she would like to poison them that have good looks."

Now Jaqueline saw that the Giant, big as he was, courageous too, was afraid of his wife!

"I'll tell you what I'll do; I'll hand you over to a neighbour of mine, who is a bachelor."

"A bachelor giant; would that be quite proper?" said Jaqueline, trying to humour him.

"He's not a giant, bless you; he's a queer fellow, it is not easy to say what he is. He's the Earthquaker, him as shakes the earth now and then, and brings the houses about people's ears."

Jaqueline fairly screamed at hearing this awful news.

"Hush! be quiet, do!" said the Giant. "You'll bring out my little woman, and she is not easy to satisfy with explanations when she finds me conversing with a lady unbeknown to her. The Earthquaker won't do you any harm; it's only for safe keeping I'll put you with him. Why, he don't waken, not once in fifty years.

He's quite the dormouse. Turns on his bed now and then, and things upstairs get upset, more or less; but, as a rule, a child could play with him. Come on!"

Then, taking Jaqueline up on one hand, on which she sat as if on a chair, he crossed a few ranges of mountains in as many strides. In front was one tall blue hill, with a flattened peak, and as they drew near the princess felt a curious kind of wind coming round her and round her. You have heard of whirlpools in water; well, this was just like a whirlpool of air. Even the Giant himself could hardly keep his legs against it; then he tossed Jaqueline up, and the airy whirlpool seized her and carried her, as if on a tide of water, always round and round in narrowing circles, till she was sucked down into the hollow hill. Even as she went, she seemed to remember the hill, as if she had dreamed about it, and the shape and colour of the country. But presently she sank softly on to a couch, in a beautifully-lighted rocky hall. All around her the floor was of white and red marble, but on one side it seemed to end in black nothing.

Jaqueline, after a few moments, recovered her senses fully, and changing herself into an eagle, tried to fly up and out. But as soon as she was in the funnel, the whirlpool of air, always sucking down and down, was too strong for her wings. She was a prisoner in this great gleaming hall, ending in black nothingness. So she resumed her usual form, and walking to the edge of the darkness, found that it was not empty air, but something black, soft, and strong —something living. It had no form or shape, or none that she could make out; but it pulsed with a heart. Jaqueline placed her foot on this curious thing, when a voice came, like thunder heard through a feather-bed:

"Not near time to get up yet!" and then there was a snore, and the great hall rocked like a ship at sea.

It was the Earthquaker!

The habits of this monstrous animal are very little known, as, of course, he never comes above ground, or at least very seldom, when he makes tracks like a dry river-bed across country. We are certain that there *are* Earthquakers, otherwise how can we account for earthquakes? But how to tackle an Earthquaker, how to get at him, and what to do with him when you have got at him, are questions which might puzzle even King Prigio.

It was not easy to have the better of an enchantress like Jaqueline and a prince like Ricardo. In no ordinary circumstances could they have been baffled and defeated; but now it must be admitted that they were in a very trying and alarming situation, especially the princess. The worst of it was, that as Jaqueline sat and thought and thought, she began to remember that she was back in her own country. The hills were those she used to see from her father's palace windows when she was a child. And she remembered with horror that once a year her people used to send a beautiful girl to the Earthquaker, by way of keeping him quiet, as you shall hear presently. And now she heard light footsteps and a sound of weeping, and lo! a great troop of pretty girls passed, sweeping in and out of the halls in a kind of procession, and looking unhappy and lost.

Jaqueline ran to them.

"Where am I? who are you?" she cried, in the language of her own country, which came back to her on a sudden.

"We are nurses of the Earthquaker," they said. "Our duty is to sing him asleep, and every year he must have a new song; and every year a new maiden must be sent down from earth, with a new sleepy song she has learned from the priests of Manoa, the City of the Sun. Are you the new singer?"

"No, I'm *not*," said Jaqueline. "I don't know the priests of Manoa; I don't know any new sleepy song. I only want to find the way out."

"There is no way, or we should have found it," said one of the maidens; "and, if you are the wrong girl, by the day after to-morrow they must send the right one, otherwise the Earthquaker will waken, and shake the world, and destroy Manoa, the City of the Sun."

Then they all wept softly in the stillness.

"Can we get anything to eat here?" asked poor Jaqueline, at last.

She was beginning to be very hungry, and however alarmed she might be, she felt that dinner would not be unwelcome. The tallest of the maidens clapped her hands, and immediately a long table was spread by unseen sprites with méringues and cold chicken, and several sorts of delicious ices.

We shall desert Jaqueline, who was rather less alarmed when she found that she was not to be starved, at all events, and return to Prince Ricardo, whom we left fluttering about as a little golden-crested wren. He followed the Giant and Jaqueline into the whirlpool of air as far as he dared, and when he saw her vanish down the cone of the hill, he flew straight back to Pantouflia.

CHAPTER IX.

Prigio Has an Idea.

A WEARY and way-worn little bird was Prince Ricardo when he fluttered into the royal study window, in the palace of Pantouflia. The king was out at a council meeting; knowing that Ricardo had the right things, all in good order, he was not in the least anxious about him. The king was out, but Semiramis was in—Semiramis, the great grey cat, sitting on a big book on the top of the library steps. Now Semiramis was very fond of birds, and no sooner did Ricardo enter and flutter on to a table than Semiramis gathered herself together and made one fell spring at him. She just caught his tail feather. In all his adventures the prince had never been in greater danger. He escaped, but no more, and went flying round the ceiling, looking for a safe place. Finally he perched on a chandelier that hung from the roof. Here he was safe; and so weary was he, that he put his head under his wing and fell fast asleep. He was awakened by the return of the king, who threw himself on a sofa and exclaimed:

"Oh, that Prime Minister! his dulness is as heavy as lead; much heavier, in fact!"

Then his Majesty lit a cigar and took up a volume; he certainly was a sad bookworm.

Dick now began to fly about the room, brushing the king's face and trying to attract his notice.

"Poor little thing!" said his Majesty.

And Dick alighted, and nestled in his breast.

On seeing this, Semiramis began to growl, as cats do when they are angry, and slowly approached his Majesty.

"Get out, Semiramis!" said the king; and lifting her by the neck, he put her out of the room and shut the door, at which she remained scratching and mewing.

Dick now crept out of the royal waistcoat, flew to the king's ear, twittered, pointed out of the window with one claw, and, lying down on his back, pretended to be dead. Then he got up again, twittered afresh, pointed to the Wishing Cap, and, finally, convinced the king that this was no common fowl.

"An enchanted prince or princess," said Prigio, "such as I have often read of. Who can it be? Not Jaqueline; she could change herself back in a moment. By the way, where *is* Jaqueline?"

He rang the bell, and asked the servant to look for the princess.

Semiramis tried to come in, but was caught and shut up downstairs.

After doing this, the man replied that her Royal Highness had not been in the palace all day.

The king rushed to the crystal ball, looked all the world over; but no princess! He became very nervous, and at that moment Dick lighted on the crystal ball, and put his claw on the very hill where Jaqueline had disappeared. Then he cocked his little eye at the king.

"Nay, she is somewhere in the unknown centre of South America," said his Majesty; "somewhere behind Mount Roraima, where nobody has ever been. I must look into this."

Then he put on the Wishing Cap, and wished that the bird would assume his natural shape if he was under enchantment, as there seemed too good reason to believe.

Instantly Dick stood before him.

"Ricardo!" cried the king in horror; "and in this disguise! Where have you been? What have you done with Jaqueline? Where are the Seven-league Boots? Where is the Sword of Sharpness? Speak! Get up!" for Dick was kneeling and weeping bitterly at the royal feet.

Instantly Dick stood before him.

"All lost!" said Dick. "Poor Jaqueline! she was the best girl, and the prettiest, and the kindest. And the Earthquaker's got her, and the Giant's got the other things," Dick ended, crying bitterly.

"Calm yourself, Ricardo," said his Majesty, very pale, but calm and determined. "Here, take a glass of port, and explain how all this happened."

Dick drank the wine, and then he told his miserable story.

"You may well sob! Why didn't you use the Cap of Darkness? Mere conceit! But there is no use in crying over spilt milk. The thing is, to rescue Jaqueline. And what are we to say to your mother?"

"That's the worst of it all," said Dick. "Mother will break her heart."

"I must see her at once," said the king, "and break it to her."

This was a terrible task; but the queen had such just confidence in her Prigio that she soon dried her tears, remarking that Heaven would not desert Jaqueline, and that the king would find a way out of the trouble.

His Majesty retired to his study, put his head in his hands, and thought and thought.

"The thing is, of course," he said, "to destroy the Earthquaker before he wakens; but how? What can kill such a monster? Prodding him with the sword would only stir him up and make him more vicious. And I know of no other beast we can set against him, as I did with the Fire-beast and the Ice-beast, when I was young. Oh, for an idea!"

Then his mind, somehow, went back to the Council and the ponderous stupidity of the Prime Minister.

"Heavier than lead," said the king. "By George! I have a plan. If I could get to the place where they keep the Stupidity, I could carry away enough of it to flatten out the Earthquaker."

Then he remembered how, in an old Italian poem, he had read about all the strange lumber-room of odd things which is kept in the moon. That is the advantage of reading: *Knowledge is Power;* and you mostly get knowledge that is really worth having out of good old books which people do not usually read.

"If the Stupidity is kept in stock, up in the moon, and comes from there, falling naturally down on the earth in small quantities, I might obtain enough for my purpose," thought King Prigio. "But — how to get to the moon? There are difficulties about that."

But difficulties only sharpened the ingenuity of this admirable king.

"The other fellow had a Flying Horse," said he.

By "the other fellow" King Prigio meant

an Italian knight, Astolfo, who, in old times, visited the moon, and there found and brought back the common sense of his friend, Orlando, as you may read in the poem of Ariosto.

"Now," reasoned King Prigio, " if there is a Flying Horse at all, he is in the stables of the King of Delhi. I must look into this."

Taking the magic spy-glass, the king surveyed the world from China to Peru, and, sure enough, there was the famous Flying Horse in the king's stable at Delhi. Hastily the king thrust his feet into the Shoes of Swiftness—so hastily, indeed, that, as the poet says, he "madly crammed a left-hand foot into a right-hand shoe." But this, many people think, is a sign of good luck; so he put the shoes on the proper feet, and in a few minutes was in the presence of the Great Mogul.

The monarch received him with some surprise, but with stately kindness, and listened to Prigio while he explained what he wanted.

"I am only too happy to assist so adventurous a prince," remarked the Great Mogul. "This is like old times! Every horse in my stable is at your service, but, as you say, only the Flying Horse is of any use to you in this expedition."

He clapped his hands, the Grand Vizier appeared, and the king gave orders to have the Flying Horse saddled at once. He then presented King Prigio with a large diamond, and came down into the courtyard to see him mount.

"He's very fresh," said the groom who held the bridle; "has not been out of the stable for three hundred years!"

Prigio sprang into the saddle among the salaams of the dusky multitude, and all the ladies of the seraglio waved their scented handkerchiefs out of the windows.

The king, as he had been instructed, turned a knob of gold in the saddle of the Flying Horse, then kissed his hand to the ladies, and, giving the steed his head, cried, in excellent Persian:

"To the moon!"

Up flew the horse with an easy action, and the king's head nearly swam with the swiftness of the flight. Soon the earth below him was no bigger than a top, spinning on its own axis (see Geography books for this), and, as night fell, earth was only a great red moon.

Through the dark rode King Prigio, into the silver dawn of the moon. All now became clear and silvery; the coasts of the moon came into sight, with white seas breaking on them; and at last the king reached the silver walls, and the gate of opal. Before the gate stood two beautiful ladies. One was fair, with yellow locks, the colour of the harvest moon. She had a crown of a golden snake and white water-lilies, and her dress now shone white,

King Prigio on the Flying Horse.

now red, now golden; and in her hand was the golden pitcher that sheds the dew, and a golden wand. The other lady was as dark as night—dark eyes, dark hair; her crown was of poppies. She held the ebony Wand of Sleep. Her dress was of the deepest blue, sown with stars. The king knew that they were the maidens of the bright and the dark side of the moon—of the side you see, and of the side that no one has ever seen, except King Prigio. He stopped the Flying Horse by turning the other knob in the saddle, alighted, and bowed very low to each of the ladies.

"Daring mortal! what make you here?" they asked.

And then the king told them about Jaqueline and the Earthquaker, and how he needed a great weight of Stupidity to flatten him out with.

The ladies heard him in silence, and then they said:

"Follow us," and they flew lightly beside the Flying Horse till they had crossed all the bright side of the moon, above the silver palaces and silver seas, and reached the summit of the Mountains of the Moon which separate the bright from the dark side.

"Here I may go no further," said the bright lady; "and beyond, as you see, all is darkness and heavy sleep."

Then she touched Prigio with her golden

wand with twisted serpents, and he became luminous, light raying out from him; and the dark lady, too, shone like silver in the night: and on they flew, over black rocks and black rivers, till they reached a huge mountain, like a mountain of coal, many thousand feet high, for its head was lost in the blackness of darkness. The dark Moon-Lady struck the rock with her ebony wand, and said, "Open!" and the cliffs opened like a door, and they were within the mountain.

"Here," said the dark lady, "is the storehouse of all the Stupidity; hence it descends in showers like stardust on the earth whenever this mountain, which is a volcano, is in eruption. Only a little of the Stupidity reaches the earth, and that only in invisible dust; yet you know how weighty it is, even in that form."

"Indeed, madam," said the king, "no one knows it better than I do."

"Then make your choice of the best sort of Stupidity for your purpose," said the dark lady.

And in the light which flowed from their bodies King Prigio looked round at the various kinds of Solid Stupidity. There it all lay in masses — the Stupidity of bad sermons, of ignorant reviewers, of bad poems, of bad speeches, of dreary novels, of foolish statesmen, of ignorant mobs, of fine ladies, of idle, naughty boys and girls; and the king examined them all, and all were very, very heavy. But when he came to the Stupidity of the Learned—of dull, blind writers on Shakspeare, and Homer, and the Bible—then King Prigio saw that he had found the sort he wanted, and that a very little of it would go a long way. He never could have got it on the saddle of the Flying Horse if the dark lady had not touched it with her ebony wand, and made it light to carry till it was wanted for his purpose. When he needed it for use, he was to utter a certain spell, which she taught him, and then the lump would recover its natural weight. So he easily put a great block on his saddle-bow, and he and the dark lady flew back till they reached the crest of the Mountains of the Moon. There she touched him with her ebony wand, and the silver light which the bright lady had shed on him died from his face and his body, and he became like other men.

"You see your way?" said the dark lady, pointing to the bright moon of earth, shining far off in the heavens.

Then he knelt down and thanked her, and she murmured strange words of blessing which he did not understand; but her face was grave and kind, and he thought of Queen Rosalind, his wife.

Then he jumped on the Flying Horse, galloped down and down, till he reached his palace gate; called for Ricardo, set him behind him on the saddle, and away they rode, above land and wide seas, till they saw the crest of the hollow hill, where Jaqueline was with the Earthquaker. Beyond it they marked the glittering spires and towers of Manoa, the City of the Sun; and "Thither," said King Prigio, who had been explaining how matters stood, to Ricardo, "we must ride, for I believe they stand in great need of our assistance."

"Had we not better go to Jaqueline first, sir?" said Ricardo.

"No," said the king; "I think mine is the best plan. Manoa, whose golden spires and pinnacles are shining below us, is the City of the Sun, which Sir Walter Raleigh and the Spaniards could never find, so that men have doubted of its existence. We are needed there, to judge by that angry crowd in the market-place. How they howl!"

CHAPTER X.

The End.

IT was on a strange sight that the king and Ricardo looked down from the Flying Horse. Beneath them lay the City of Manoa, filling with its golden battlements and temples a hollow of the mountains. Here were palaces all carved over with faces of men and beasts, and with twisted patterns of serpents. The city walls were built of huge square stones, and among the groves towered pyramids, on which the people did service to their gods. From every temple top came the roar of beaten drums, great drums of serpentskin.

But, in the centre of the chief square of the town, was gathered a wild crowd of men in shining copper armour and helmets of gold and glittering dresses of feathers. Among them ran about priests with hideous masks, crying them on to besiege and break down the royal palace. From the battlements of the palace the king's guardsmen were firing arrows and throwing spears. The mob shot arrows back, some of them tipped with lighted straw, to burn the palace down.

But, in the very centre of the square, was a clear space of ground, on which fell the shadow of a tall column of red stone, all carved with serpents and faces of gods. Beside it stood a figure horrible to see: a man clothed in serpent skins, whose face was the grinning face of a skull; but the skull was shining black and red in patches, and a long white beard flowed from beneath it. This man, mounted on a kind of altar of red stone, waved his hand and yelled, and seemed to point to the shadow of the column which fell across the square.

The people were so furious and so eager that they did not, at first, notice King Prigio as he slowly descended. But at last the eyes within the skull looked up and saw him, and then the man gave a great cry, rent his glittering dress of serpentskin, and held up his hands.

Then all the multitude looked up, and seeing the Flying Horse, let their weapons fall; and the man of the skull tore it from his face, and knelt before King Prigio, with his head in the dust.

"Thou hast come, oh, Pachacamac, as is foretold in the prophecy of the Cord of the Venerable Knots! Thou hast come, but behold the shadow of the stone! Thou art too late, oh Lord of the Earth and the Sea!"

Then he pointed to the shadow, which, naturally, was growing shorter, as the sun drew near mid-day.

He spoke in the language of the ancient Incas of Peru, which of course Prigio knew very well; and he also knew that Pachacamac was the god of that people.

"I have come," Prigio said, with presence of mind, "as it has been prophesied of old."

"Riding on a beast that flies," said the old priest, "even as the oracle declared. Glory to Pachacamac, even though we die to-day!"

"In what can I help my people?" said Prigio.

"Thou knowest; why should we instruct thee? Thou knowest that on midsummer-day, every year, before the shadow shrinks back to the base of the *huaca** of Manoa, we must offer a maiden to lull the Earthquaker with a new song. Lo, now the shadow shrinks to the foot of the *huaca*, and the maid is not offered! For the lot fell on the daughter of thy servant the

* *Huaca*, sacred stone.

Inca, and he refuses to give her up. One daughter of his, he says, has been sacrificed to the sacred birds, the *Cunturs:* the birds were found slain on the hill-top, no man knows how; but the maiden vanished.

"Why, it must have been Jaqueline. I killed the birds," said Ricardo, in Pantouflian.

"Silence, not a word!" said the king, sternly.

"And what makes you bear arms against the Inca?" he asked the old man.

"We would slay him and her," answered the priest; "for, when the shadow shrinks to the foot of the stone, the sun will shine straight down into the hollow hill of the Earthquaker, and he will waken and destroy Manoa and the Temples of the Sun."

"Then wherefore would you slay them, when you must all perish?"

"The people, oh Pachacamac, would have revenge before they die."

"Oh, folly of men!" said the king, solemnly; then he cried: "Lead me to the Inca; this day you shall not perish. Is it not predicted in the Cord of the Venerable Knots that I shall slay this monster?"

"Hasten, oh Pachacamac, for the shadow shortens!" said the priest.

"Lead me to the Inca," answered Prigio.

At this the people arose with a great shout,

for they, too, had been kneeling; and, sending a flag of truce before King Prigio, the priest led him into the palace. The ground was strewn with bodies of the slain, and through them Prigio rode slowly into the courtyard, where the Inca was sitting in the dust, weeping and throwing ashes on his long hair and his golden raiment. The king bade the priest remain without the palace gates; then dismounted, and, advancing to the Inca, raised him and embraced him.

"I come, a king to a king," he said. "My cousin, take courage; your sorrows are ended. If I do not slay the Earthquaker, sacrifice me to your gods."

"The Prophecy is fulfilled," said the Inca, and wept for joy. "Yet thou must hasten, for it draws near to noon."

Then Prigio went up to the golden battlements, and saying no word, waved his hand. In a moment the square was empty, for the people rushed to give thanks in the temples.

"Wait my coming, my cousin," said Prigio to the Inca; "I shall bring you back the daughter that was lost, when I have slain your enemy."

The Inca would have knelt at his feet; but the king raised him, and bade him prepare such a feast as had never been seen in Manoa.

"The lost are found to-day," he said; "be you ready to welcome them."

Then, mounting the Flying Horse, with Dick beside him, he rose towards the peak of the hill where the Earthquaker had his home. Already the ground was beginning to tremble; the Earthquaker was stirring in his sleep, for the maiden of the new song had not been sent to him, and the year ended at noon, and then he would rise and ruin Manoa.

The sun was approaching mid-day, and Prigio put spurs to the Flying Horse. Ten minutes more, and the sun would look straight down the crater of the hollow hill, and the Earthquaker would arouse himself when the light and the heat fell on his body.

Already the light of the sun shone slanting half-way down the hollow cone as the whirlpool of air caught the Flying Horse, and drew him swiftly down and down to the shadowy halls. There knelt and wept the nurses of the Earthquaker on the marble floor; but Jaqueline stood a little apart, very pale, but not weeping.

Ricardo had leaped off before the horse touched the ground, and rushed to Jaqueline, and embraced her in his arms; and, oh! how glad she was to see him, so that she quite forgot her danger and laughed for joy.

"Oh! you have come, you have come; I knew you would come!" she cried.

Then King Prigio advanced, the mighty weight in his hand, to the verge of the dreadful gulf of the Earthquaker. The dim walls grew radiant; a long slant arm of yellow light touched the black body of the Earthquaker, and a thrill went through him, and shook the world, so that, far away, the bells rang in Pantouflia. A moment more, and he would waken in his strength; and once awake, he would shatter the city walls, and ruin Manoa. Even now a great mass of rock fell from the roof deep down in the secret caves, and broke into flying fragments, and all the echoes roared and rang.

King Prigio stood with the mighty mass poised in his hands.

"Die!" he cried; and he uttered the words of power, the magic spell that the dark Moon Lady had taught him.

Then all its invincible natural weight came into the mass which the king held, and down it shot full on the body of the Earthquaker; and where that had been was nothing but a vast abyss, silent, empty, and blank, and bottomless.

Far, far below, thousands of miles below, in the very centre of the earth, lay the dead Earthquaker, crushed flat as a sheet of paper, and the sun of midsummer-day shone straight down on the dreadful chasm, and could not waken him any more for ever.

The king drew a long breath.

"Stupidity has saved the world," he said; and, with only strength to draw back one step from the abyss, he fell down, hiding his face in his hands.

But Jaqueline's arms were round his neck, and the maidens brought him water from an ice-cold spring; and soon King Prigio was himself again, and ready for anything. But afterwards he used to say that the moment when the Earthquaker stirred was the most dreadful in his life.

Now, in Manoa, where all the firm foundations of the city had trembled once, when the sun just touched the Earthquaker, the people, seeing that the shadow of the sacred column had crept to its foot, and yet Manoa stood firm again, and the Temple of the Sun was not overthrown, raised such a cry that it echoed even through the halls within the hollow hill.

Who shall describe the joy of the maidens, and how often Jaqueline and Ricardo kissed each other?

"You have saved me!" she cried to the king, throwing her arms round him again. "You have saved Manoa!"

"And *you* have saved the Hope of Pantouflia, not once or twice," said his Majesty, grandly.

And he told Dick how much he had owed to

Jaqueline, in the fight with the Yellow Dwarf, and the fight with the Giant, for he did not think it necessary to mention the affair at Rome.

Then Dick kissed Jaqueline again, and all the maidens kissed each other, and they quite cried for gladness.

"But we keep his Majesty the Inca waiting," said Prigio. "Punctuality is the courtesy of kings. You ladies will excuse me, I am sure, if I remove first from the dungeon her whom we call the Princess Jaqueline. The Inca, her father, has a claim on us to this preference."

Then placing Jaqueline on the saddle, and leaving Dick to comfort the other young ladies, who were still rather nervous, the king flew off to Manoa, for the wind, of course, died with the death of the Earthquaker.

I cannot tell you the delight of all Manoa, and of the Inca, when they saw the Flying Horse returning, and recognised their long-lost princess, who rushed into the arms of her father. They beat the serpent drums, for they had no bells, on the tops of the temples. They went quite mad with delight: enemies kissed in the streets; and all the parents, without exception, allowed all the young people who happened to be in love to be married that very day. Then Prigio brought back all the maidens, one after the other, and Dick last; and he fell at the Inca's feet, and requested leave to marry Jaqueline.

But, before that could be done, King Prigio, mounted on the palace balcony, made a long but very lucid speech to the assembled people. He began by explaining that he was not their God, Pachacamac, but king of a powerful country of which they had never heard before, as they lived very much withdrawn in an unknown region of the world. Then he pointed out, in the most considerate manner, that their religion was not all he could wish, otherwise they would never sacrifice young ladies to wild birds and Earthquakers. He next sketched out the merits of his own creed, that of the Lutheran Church; and the Inca straightway observed that he proposed to establish it in Manoa at once.

Some objection was raised by the old priest in the skull mask; but when the Inca promised to make him an archbishop, and to continue all his revenues, the priest admitted that he was perfectly satisfied; and the general public cheered and waved their hats with emotion. It was arranged that the Inca, with his other daughters, should visit Pantouflia immediately, both because he could not bear to leave Jaqueline, and also because there were a few points on which he felt that he still needed information. The Government was left in the hands of the archbishop, who began at once by burning his skull mask (you may see one like it in the British Museum, in the Mexican room), and by letting loose all the birds and beasts which the Manoans used to worship.

So all the young people were married in the Golden Temple of the Sun, and all the Earthquaker's nurses who were under thirty were wedded to the young men who had been fond of them before they were sent into the hollow hill. These young men had never cared for any one else. Everybody wore bridal favours, all the unengaged young ladies acted as bridesmaids, and such a throwing of rice and old shoes has very seldom been witnessed. As for the happy royal pair, with their fathers, and the other princess (who did not happen to be engaged), back they flew to Pantouflia.

And there was Queen Rosalind waiting at the palace gates, and crying and laughing with pleasure when she heard that the wish of her heart was fulfilled, and Jaqueline was to be her daughter.

"And, as for the Earthquaker," said her Majesty, "I never was really anxious in the least, for I knew no beast in the world was a match for *you*, my dear."

So, just to make everything orderly and correct, Ricardo and Jaqueline were married over again, in the Cathedral of Pantouflia. The marriage presents came in afterwards, of course, and among them, what do you think? Why, the Seven-League Boots and the Sword of Sharpness, with a very polite note of extraordinary size:

"The Giant who does not Know when he has had Enough presents his hearty congratulations to the royal pair, and begs to lay at their feet the Seven-league Boots (they not fitting me) and the Sword which Prince Ricardo left in the Giant's keeping recently. The Giant hopes *no bad blood;* and I am,

"Yours very faithfully,
"The G., &c.

"P.S.—His little woman sends her congratulations."

So you see the Giant was not such a bad sort of fellow after all, and Prince Ricardo always admitted that he never met a foe more gallant and good-humoured.

With such a clever wife, Ricardo easily passed all his examinations; and his little son, Prince Prigio (named after his august grandfather), never had to cry, "Mamma, mamma, father's plucked again."

So they lived happily in a happy country, occasionally visiting Manoa; and as they possessed the magical Water of Life from the Fountain of Lions, I do not believe that any of them ever died at all, but that Prigio is still King of Pantouflia.

"No need such kings should ever die!"

THE GOLD OF FAIRNILEE

THE GOLD OF FAIRNILEE

IS

Dedicated

TO

JEANIE LANG,

LARRA

Dear Jeanie,

For you, far away on the other side of the world, I made this little tale of our own country. Your father and I have dug for treasure in the Camp of Rink, with our knives, when we were boys. We did not find it: the story will tell you why.

Are there Fairies as well as Bunyips in Australia? I hope so.

Yours always,

A. Lang.

WHUPPITY STOORIE'S SONG

IN THIS TALE

IS BY THE AUTHOR'S FRIEND,

F. De Q. M.

The Old House.

The Gold of Fairnilee.

CHAPTER I.

The Old House.

YOU may still see the old Scotch house where Randal was born, so long ago. Nobody lives there now. Most of the roof has fallen in, there is no glass in the windows, and all the doors are open. They were open in the days of Randal's father — nearly four hundred years have passed since then — and everyone who came was welcome to his share of beef and broth and ale. But now the doors are not only open, they are quite gone, and there is nobody within to give you a welcome.

So there is nothing but emptiness in the old house where Randal lived with Jean, three hundred and sixty years or so before you were born. It is a high old house, and wide, with the broken slates still on the roof. At the corner there are little round towers, like pepper-boxes, with sharp peaks. The stems of the ivy that covers the walls are as thick as trees. There are many trees crowding all round, and there are hills round it too; and far below you hear the Tweed whispering all day. The house is called Fairnilee, which means "the Fairies' Field;" for people believed in fairies, as you shall hear, when Randal was a boy, and even when my father was a boy.

Randal was all alone in the house when he was a little fellow—alone with his mother, and Nancy the old nurse, and Simon Grieve the butler, who wore a black velvet coat and a big silver chain. Then there were the maids, and the grooms, and the farm folk, who were all friends of Randal's. He was not lonely, and he did not feel unhappy, even before Jean came, as you shall be told. But the grown-up people were sad and silent at Fairnilee. Randal had no father; his mother, Lady Ker, was a widow. She was still quite young, and Randal thought her the most beautiful person in the world. Children think these things about their mothers, and Randal had seen no ladies but his mother only. She had brown hair and brown eyes and red lips, and a grave kind face, which looked serious under her great white widow's cap with the black hood over it. Randal never saw his mother cry; but when he was a very little child indeed, he had heard her crying in the night: this was after his father went away.

CHAPTER II.

How Randal's Father Came Home.

RANDAL remembered his father's going to fight the English, and how he came back again. It was a windy August evening when he went away: the rain had fallen since morning. Randal had watched the white mists driven by the gale down through the black pine-wood that covers the hill opposite Fairnilee. The mist looked like armies of ghosts, he thought, marching, marching through the pines, with their white flags flying and streaming. Then the sun came out red at evening, and Randal's father rode away with all his men. He had a helmet on his head, and a great axe hanging from his neck by a chain, and a spear in his hand. He was riding his big horse, *Sir Hugh*, and he caught Randal up to the saddle and kissed him many times before he clattered out of the courtyard. All the tenants and men about the farm rode with him, all with spears and a flag embroidered with a crest in gold. His mother watched them from the tower till they were out of sight. And Randal saw them ride away, not on hard, smooth roads like ours, but along a green grassy track, the water splashing up to their stirrups where they crossed the marshes.

Then the sky turned as red as blood, in the sunset, and next it grew brown, like the rust on a sword; and the Tweed below, when they rode the ford, was all red and gold and brown.

Then time went on; that seemed a long time to Randal. Only the women were left in the house, and Randal played with the shepherd's children. They sailed boats in the mill-pond, and they went down to the boat-pool and watched to see the big copper-coloured salmon splashing in the still water. One evening Randal looked up suddenly from his play. It was growing dark. He had been building a house with the round stones and wet sand by the river. He looked up, and there was his own father! He was riding all alone, and his horse, *Sir Hugh*, was very lean and lame, and scarred with the spurs. The spear in his father's hand was broken, and he had no sword; and he looked neither to right nor to left. His eyes were wide open, but he seemed to see nothing.

Randal cried out to him, "Father! Father!" but he never glanced at Randal. He did not look as if he heard him, or knew he was there, and suddenly he seemed to go away, Randal did not know how or where.

Randal was frightened.

He ran into the house, and went to his mother.

"Oh, mother," he said, "I have seen father! He was riding all alone, and he would not look at me. *Sir Hugh* was lame!"

"Where has he gone?" said Lady Ker, in a strange voice.

"He went away out of sight," said Randal. "I could not see where he went."

Then his mother told him it could not be, that his father would not have come back alone. He would not leave his men behind him in the war.

But Randal was so sure, that she did not scold him. She knew he believed what he said.

He saw that she was not happy.

All that night, which was the Fourth of September, in the year 1513, the day of Flodden fight, Randal's mother did not go to bed. She kept moving about the house. Now she would look from the tower window up Tweed; and now she would go along the gallery and look down Tweed from the other tower. She had lights burning in all the windows. All next day she was never still. She climbed, with two of her maids, to the top of the hill above Yair, on the other side of the river, and she watched the roads down Ettrick and Yarrow. Next night she slept little, and rose early. About noon, Randal saw three or four men riding wearily, with tired horses. They could scarcely cross the ford of Tweed, the horses were so tired. The men were Simon Grieve the butler, and some of the tenants. They looked very pale; some of them had their heads tied up, and there was blood on their faces. Lady Ker and Randal ran to meet them.

Simon Grieve lighted from his horse, and whispered to Randal's mother.

Randal did not hear what he said, but his mother cried, "I knew it! I knew it!" and turned quite white.

"Where is he?" she said.

Simon pointed across the hill. "They are bringing the corp," he said. Randal knew the "corp" meant the dead body.

He began to cry. "Where is my father?" he said, "where is my father?"

His mother led him into the house. She gave him to the old nurse, who cried over him, and kissed him, and offered him cakes, and made him a whistle with a branch of plane tree. So in a short while Randal only felt puzzled. Then he forgot, and began to play. He was a very little boy.

Lady Ker shut herself up in her own room— her "bower," the servants called it.

Soon Randal heard heavy steps on the stairs, and whispering. He wanted to run out, and his nurse caught hold of him, and would not have let him go, but he slipped out of her hand, and looked over the staircase.

They were bringing up the body of a man stretched on a shield.

It was Randal's father.

He had been slain at Flodden, fighting for the king. An arrow had gone through his brain, and he had fallen beside James IV., with many another brave knight, all the best of Scotland, the Flowers of the Forest.

What was it Randal saw, when he thought he met his father in the twilight, three days before?

He never knew. His mother said he must have dreamed it all.

The old nurse used to gossip about it to the maids. "He's an unco' bairn, oor Randal; I wush he may na be fey."

She meant that Randal was a strange child, and that strange things would happen to him.

CHAPTER III.

How Jean was brought to Fairnilee.

THE winter went by very sadly. At first the people about Fairnilee expected the English to cross the Border and march against them. They drove their cattle out on the wild hills, and into marshes where only they knew the firm paths, and raised walls of earth and stones—*barmkyns*, they called them—round the old house; and made many arrows to shoot out of the narrow windows at the English. Randal used to like to see the arrow-making beside the fire at night. He was not afraid; and said he would show the English what he could do with his little bow. But weeks went on and no enemy came.  Spring drew near, the snow melted from the hills. One night Randal was awakened by a great noise of shouting; he looked out of the window, and saw bright torches moving about. He heard the cows "routing," or bellowing, and the women screaming. He thought the English had come. So they had; not the English army, but some robbers from the other side of the Border. At that time the people on the south side of Scotland and the north side of England used to steal each other's cows time about. When a Scotch squire, or "laird," like Randal's father, had been robbed by the neighbouring English, he would wait his chance and drive away cattle from the English side. This time most of Randal's mother's herds were seized, by a sudden attack in the night, and were driven away through the Forest to England. Two or three of Lady Ker's men were hurt by the English, but old Simon Grieve took a prisoner. He did this in a curious way. He shot an arrow after the robbers as they rode off, and the arrow pinned an Englishman's leg to the saddle, and even into his horse. The horse was hurt and frightened, and ran away right back to Fairnilee, where it was caught, with the rider and all, for of course he could not dismount.

They treated him kindly at Fairnilee, though they laughed at him a good deal. They found out from him where the English had come from. He did not mind telling them, for he was really a gipsy from Yetholm, where the gipsies live, and Scot or Southron was all one to him.

When old Simon Grieve knew who the people were that had taken the cows, he was not long in calling the men together, and trying to get back what he had lost. Early one April morning, a grey morning, with snow in the air, he and his spearmen set out, riding down through the Forest, and so into Liddesdale. When they came back again, there were great rejoicings at Fairnilee. They drove most of their own cows before them, and a great many other cows that they had not lost; cows of the English farmers. The byres and yards were soon full of cattle, lowing and roaring, very uneasy, and some of them with marks of the spears that had goaded them across many a ford, and up many a rocky pass in the hills.

Randal jumped downstairs to the great hall, where his mother sat. Simon Grieve was telling her all about it.

"Sae we drave oor ain kye hame, my lady," he said, "and aiblins some orra anes that was na oor ain. For-bye we raikit a' the plenishing oot o' the ha' o' Hardriding, and a bonny burden o' tapestries, and plaids, and gear we hae, to show for our ride."*

* "We drove our own cattle home, and perhaps some others that were not ours. And we took all the goods out of the hall at Hardriding, and a pretty load of tapestries, and rugs, and other things we have to show for our ride."

Then he called to some of his men, who came into the hall, and cast down great piles of all sorts of spoil and booty, silver plate, and silken hangings, and a heap of rugs, and carpets, and plaids, such as Randal had never seen before, for the English were much richer than the Scotch.

Randal threw himself on the pile of rugs and began to roll on it.

"Oh, mother," he cried suddenly, jumping up and looking with wide-open eyes, "there's something living in the heap! Perhaps it's a doggie, or a rabbit, or a kitten."

Then Randal tugged at the cloths, and then they all heard a little shrill cry.

"Why, it's a bairn!" said Lady Ker, who had sat very grave all the time, pleased to have done the English some harm; for they had killed her husband, and were all her deadly foes. "It's a bairn!" she cried, and pulled out of the great heap of cloaks and rugs a little beautiful child, in its white nightdress, with its yellow curls all tangled over its blue eyes.

Then Lady Ker and the old nurse could not make too much of the pretty English child that had come here in such a wonderful way.

How did it get mixed up with all the spoil? and how had it been carried so far on horseback without being hurt? Nobody ever knew. It came as if the fairies had sent it. English it was, but the best Scot could not hate such a pretty child. Old Nancy Dryden ran up to the old nursery with it, and laid it in a great wooden tub full of hot water, and was giving it warm milk to drink, and dandling it, almost before the men knew what had happened.

"Yon bairn will be a bonny mate for you, Maister Randal," said old Simon Grieve. "'Deed, I dinna think her kin will come speering* after her at Fairnilee. The Red Cock's crawing ower Hardriding Ha' this day,

* Asking.

and when the womenfolk come back frae the wood, they'll hae other thing to do for-bye looking for bairns."

When Simon Grieve said that the Red Cock was crowing over his enemies' home, he meant that he had set it on fire after the people who lived in it had run away.

Lady Ker grew pale when she heard what he said. She hated the English, to be sure, but she was a woman with a kind heart. She thought of the dreadful danger that the little English girl had escaped, and she went upstairs and helped the nurse to make the child happy.

CHAPTER IV.

Randal and Jean.

THE little girl soon made everyone at Fairnilee happy. She was far too young to remember her own home, and presently she was crawling up and down the long hall and making friends with Randal. They found out that her name was Jane Musgrave, though she could hardly say Musgrave; and they called her Jean, with their Scotch tongues, or "Jean o' the Kye," because she came when the cows were driven home again.

Soon the old nurse came to like her near as well as Randal, "her ain bairn" (her own child), as she called him. In the summer days, Jean, as she grew older, would follow Randal about like a little doggie. They went fishing together, and Randal would pull the trout out of Caddon Burn, or the Burn of Peel; and Jeanie would be very proud of him, and very much alarmed at the big, wide jaws of the yellow trout. And Randal would plait helmets with green rushes for her and him, and make spears of bulrushes, and play at tilts and tournaments. There was peace in the country; or if there was war, it did not come near the quiet valley of the Tweed and the hills that lie round Fairnilee. In summer they were always on the hills and by the burnsides.

You cannot think, if you have not tried, what pleasant company a burn is. It comes out of the deep, black wells in the moss, far away on the tops of the hills, where the sheep feed, and the fox peers from his hole, and the ravens build in the crags. The burn flows down from the lonely places, cutting a way between steep, green banks, tumbling in white waterfalls over rocks, and lying in black, deep pools below the waterfalls. At every turn it does something new, and plays a fresh game with its brown waters. The white pebbles in the water look like gold: often Randal would pick one out and think he had found a gold-mine, till he got it into the sunshine, and then it was only a white stone, what he called a "chucky-stane;" but he kept hoping for better luck next time. In the height of summer, when the streams were very low, he and the shepherd's boys would build dams of stones and turf across a narrow part of the burn, while Jean sat and watched them on a little round knoll. Then, when plenty of water had collected in the pool, they would break the dam and let it all run downhill in a little flood; they called it a "hurly gush." And in winter they would slide on the black, smooth ice of the boat-pool, beneath the branches of the alders.

Or they would go out with *Yarrow*, the shepherd's dog, and follow the track of wild creatures in the snow. The rabbit makes marks like ∴, and the hare makes marks like ∷ ; but the fox's track is just as if you had pushed a piece of wood through the snow —a number of cuts in the surface, going straight along. When it was very cold, the grouse and black-cocks would come into the trees near the house, and Randal and Jean would put out porridge for them to eat. And the great white swans floated in from the frozen lochs on the hills, and gathered round open reaches and streams of the Tweed. It was pleasant to be a boy then in the North. And at Hallow E'en they would duck for apples in tubs of water, and burn nuts in the fire, and look for the shadow of the lady Randal was to marry, in the mirror; but he only saw Jean looking over his shoulder.

The days were very short in winter, so far North, and they would soon be driven into the house. Then they sat by the nursery fire; and those were almost the pleasantest hours, for the old nurse would tell them old Scotch stories of elves and fairies, and sing them old songs. Jean would crawl close to Randal and hold his hand, for fear the Red Etin, or some other awful bogle, should get her: and in the dancing shadows of the firelight she would think she saw Whuppity Stoorie, the wicked old witch with the spinning-wheel; but it was

really nothing but the shadow of the wheel that the old nurse drove with her foot—*birr, birr*—and that whirred and rattled as she span and told her tale. For people span their cloth at home then, instead of buying it from shops; and the old nurse was a great woman for spinning.

She was a great woman for stories, too, and believed in fairies, and "bogles," as she called them. Had not her own cousin, Andrew Tamson, passed the Cauldshiels Loch one New Year morning? And had he not heard a dreadful roaring, as if all the cattle on Faldonside Hill were routing at once? And then did he not see a great black beast roll down the hillside, like a black ball, and run into the loch, which grew white with foam, and the waves leaped up the banks like a tide rising? What could that be except the kelpie that lives in Cauldshiels Loch, and is just a muckle big water bull? "And what for should there no be water kye, if there's land kye?"

Randal and Jean thought it was very likely there were "kye," or cattle, in the water. And some Highland people think so still, and believe they have seen the great kelpie come roaring out of the lake; or Shellycoat, whose skin is all crusted like a rock with shells, sitting beside the sea.

The old nurse had other tales, that nobody believes any longer, about Brownies. A Brownie was a very useful creature to have in a house. He was a kind of fairy-man, and he came out in the dark, when everybody had gone to bed, just as mice pop out at night.

He never did anyone any harm, but he sat and warmed himself at the kitchen fire. If any work was unfinished he did it, and made everything tidy that was left out of order. It is a pity there are no such bogles now! If anybody offered the Brownie any payment, even if it was only a silver penny or a new coat, he would take offence and go away.

Other stories the old nurse had, about hidden treasures and buried gold. If you believed her, there was hardly an old stone on the hillside but had gold under it. The very sheep that fed upon the Eildon Hills, which Randal knew well, had yellow teeth because there was so much gold under the grass. Randal had taken two scones, or rolls, in his pocket for dinner, and ridden over to the Eildon Hills. He had seen a rainbow touch one of them, and there he hoped he would find the treasure that always lies at the tail of the rainbow. But he got very soon tired of digging for it with his little dirk, or dagger. It blunted the dagger, and he found nothing. Perhaps he had not marked quite the right place, he thought. But he looked at the teeth of the sheep, and they were yellow; so he had no doubt that there was a gold-mine under the grass, if he could find it.

The old nurse knew that it was very difficult to dig up fairy gold. Generally something happened just when people heard their pickaxes clink on the iron pot that held the treasure. A dreadful storm of thunder and lightning would break out; or the burn would be flooded, and rush down all red and roaring, sweeping away the tools and drowning the digger; or a strange man, that nobody had ever seen before, would come up, waving his arms, and crying out that the Castle was on fire. Then the people would hurry up to the Castle, and find that it was not on fire at all. When they returned, all the earth would be just as it was before they began, and they would give up in despair. Nobody could ever see the man again that gave the alarm.

"Who could he be, nurse?" Randal asked.

"Just one of the good folk, I'm thinking; but it's no weel to be speaking o' *them*."

Randal knew that the "good folk" meant the fairies. The old nurse called them the good folk for fear of offending them. She would not speak much about them, except now and then, when the servants had been making merry.

"And is there any treasure hidden near Fairnilee, nursie?" asked little Jean.

"Treasure, my bonny doo! Mair than a' the men about the toon could carry away frae morning till nicht. Do ye no ken the auld rhyme?—

> 'Atween the wet ground and the dry
> The gold of Fairnilee doth lie.'

And there's the other auld rhyme—

> 'Between the Camp o' Rink
> And Tweed water clear,
> Lie nine kings' ransoms
> For nine hundred year!'"

Randal and Jean were very glad to hear so much gold was near them as would pay nine kings' ransoms. They took their small spades and dug little holes in the Camp of Rink, which is a great old circle of stonework, surrounded by a deep ditch, on the top of a hill above the house. But Jean was not a very good digger, and even Randal grew tired. They thought they would wait till they grew bigger, and *then* find the gold.

CHAPTER V.

The Good Folk.

"EVERYBODY knows there's fairies," said the old nurse one night when she was bolder than usual. What she said we will put in English, not Scotch as she spoke it. "But they do not like to be called fairies. So the old rhyme runs:

> 'If ye call me imp or elf,
> I warn you look well to yourself;
> If ye call me fairy,
> Ye'll find me quite contrary;
> If good neighbour you call me,
> Then good neighbour I will be;
> But if you call me kindly sprite,
> I'll be your friend both day and night.'

So you must always call them 'good neighbours' or 'good folk,' when you speak of them."

"Did *you* ever see a fairy, nurse?" asked Randal.

"Not myself, but my mother knew a woman —they called her Tibby Dickson, and her husband was a shepherd, and she had a bairn, as bonny a bairn as ever you saw. And one day she went to the well to draw water, and as she was coming back she heard a loud scream in her house. Then her heart leaped, and fast she ran and flew to the cradle; and there she saw an awful sight—not her own bairn, but a withered imp, with hands like a mole's, and a face like a frog's, and a mouth from ear to ear, and two great staring eyes."

"What was it?" asked Jeanie, in a trembling voice.

"A fairy's bairn that had not thriven," said nurse; "and when their bairns do not thrive, they just steal honest folks' children and carry them away to their own country."

"And where's that?" said Randal.

"It's under the ground," said nurse, "and there they have gold and silver and diamonds; and there's the Queen of them all, that's as beautiful as the day. She has yellow hair down to her feet, and she has blue eyes, like the sky on a fine day, and her voice like all the mavises singing in the spring. And she is aye dressed in green, and all her court in green; and she rides a white horse with golden bells on the bridle."

"I would like to go there and see her," said Randal.

"Oh, never say that, my bairn; you never know who may hear you! And if you go there, how will you come back again? and what will your mother do, and Jean here, and me that's carried you many a time in weary arms when you were a babe?"

"Can't people come back again?" asked Randal.

"Some say 'Yes,' and some say 'No.' There was Tam Hislop, that vanished away the day before all the lads and your own father went forth to that weary war at Flodden, and the English, for once, by guile, won the day. Well, Tam Hislop, when the news came that all must arm and mount and ride, he could nowhere be found. It was as if the wind had carried him away. High and low they sought him, but there was his clothes and his jack,* and his sword and his spear, but no Tam Hislop. Well, no man heard more of him for seven whole years, not till last year, and then he came back: sore tired he looked, ay, and older than when he was lost. And I met him by the well, and I was frightened; and 'Tam,' I said, 'where have ye been this weary time?' 'I have been with them that I will not speak the name of,' says he. 'Ye mean the good folk,' said I. 'Ye have said it,' says he. Then I went up to the house, with my heart in my mouth, and I met Simon Grieve. 'Simon,' I says, 'here's Tam Hislop come home from the good folk.' 'I'll soon send him back to them,' says he. And he takes a great rung† and lays it about Tam's shoulders, calling him coward

* Jack, a kind of breastplate. † Rung, a staff.

loon, that ran away from the fighting. And since then Tam has never been seen about the place. But the Laird's man, of Gala, knows them that say he was in Perth the last seven years, and not in Fairyland at all. But it was Fairyland he told me, and he would not lie to his own mother's half-brother's cousin."

Randal did not care much for the story of Tam Hislop. A fellow who would let old Simon Grieve beat him could not be worthy of the Fairy Queen.

Randal was about thirteen now, a tall boy, with dark eyes, black hair, a brown face with the red on his cheeks. He had grown up in a country where everything was magical and haunted; where fairy knights rode on the leas after dark, and challenged men to battle. Every castle had its tale of Redcap, the sly spirit, or of the woman of the hairy hand. Every old mound was thought to cover hidden gold. And all was so lonely; the green hills rolling between river and river, with no men on them, nothing but sheep, and grouse, and plover. No wonder that Randal lived in a kind of dream. He would lie and watch the long grass till it looked like a forest, and he thought he could see elves dancing between the green grass stems, that were like fairy trees. He kept wishing that he, too, might meet the Fairy Queen, and be taken into that other world where everything was beautiful.

CHAPTER VI.

The Wishing Well.

"JEAN," said Randal one midsummer day, "I am going to the Wishing Well."

"Oh, Randal," said Jean, "it is so far away!"

"I can walk it," said Randal, "and you must come, too; I want you, Jeanie. It's not so very far."

"But mother says it is wrong to go to Wishing Wells," Jean answered.

"Why is it wrong?" said Randal, switching at the tall foxgloves with a stick.

"Oh, she says it is a wicked thing, and forbidden by the Church. People who go to wish there, sacrifice to the spirits of the well; and Father Francis told her that it was very wrong."

"Father Francis is a shaveling," said Randal. "I heard Simon Grieve say so."

"What's a shaveling, Randal?"

"I don't know: a man that does not fight, I think. I don't care what a shaveling says: so I mean just to go and wish, and I won't sacrifice anything. There can't be any harm in *that!*"

"But, oh Randal, you've got your green doublet on!"

"Well! why not?"

"Do you not know it angers the fair—I mean the good folk,—that anyone should wear green on the hill but themselves?"

"I cannot help it," said Randal. "If I go in and change my doublet, they will ask what I do that for. I'll chance it, green or grey, and wish my wish for all that."

"And what are you going to wish?"

"I'm going to wish to meet the Fairy Queen! Just think how beautiful she must be! dressed all in green, with gold bells on her bridle, and riding a white horse shod with gold! I think I see her galloping through the woods and out across the hill, over the heather."

"But you will go away with her, and never see me any more," said Jean.

"No, I won't; or if I do, I'll come back, with such a horse, and a sword with a gold handle. I'm going to the Wishing Well. Come on!"

Jean did not like to say "No," and off they went.

Randal and Jean started without taking anything with them to eat. They were afraid to go back to the house for food. Randal said they would be sure to find something somewhere. The Wishing Well was on the top of a hill between Yarrow and Tweed. So they took off their shoes, and waded the Tweed at the shallowest part, and then they walked up the green grassy bank on the other side, till

they came to the burn of Peel. Here they passed the old square tower of Peel, and the shepherd dogs came out and barked at them. Randal threw a stone at them, and they ran away with their tails between their legs.

"Don't you think we had better go into Peel, and get some bannocks to eat on the way, Randal?" said Jean.

But Randal said he was not hungry; and, besides, the people at Peel would tell the Fairnilee people where they had gone.

"We'll *wish* for things to eat when we get to the Wishing Well," said Randal. "All sorts of good things—cold venison pasty, and everything you like."

So they began climbing the hill, and they followed the Peel burn. It ran in and out, winding this way and that, and when they did get to the top of the hill, Jean was very tired and very hungry. And she was very disappointed. For she expected to see some wonderful new country at her feet, and there was only a low strip of sunburnt grass and heather, and then another hill-top! So Jean sat down, and the hot sun blazed on her, and the flies buzzed about her and tormented her.

"Come on, Jean," said Randal; "it must be over the next hill!"

So poor Jean got up and followed him, but he walked far too fast for her. When she reached the crest of the next hill, she found a great cairn, or pile of grey stones; and beneath her lay, far, far below, a deep valley covered with woods, and a stream running through it that she had never seen before.

That stream was the Yarrow.

Randal was nowhere in sight, and she did not know where to look for the Wishing Well. If she had walked straight forward through the trees she would have come to it; but she was so tired, and so hungry, and so hot, that she sat down at the foot of the cairn and cried as if her heart would break.

Then she fell asleep.

When Jean woke, it was as dark as it ever is on a midsummer night in Scotland.

It was a soft, cloudy night; not a clear night with a silver sky.

Jeanie heard a loud roaring close to her, and the red light of a great fire was in her sleepy eyes.

In the firelight she saw strange black beasts, with horns, plunging and leaping and bellowing, and dark figures rushing about the flames. It was the beasts that made the roaring. They

were bounding about close to the fire, and sometimes in it, and were all mixed in the smoke.

Jeanie was dreadfully frightened, too frightened to scream.

Presently she heard the voices of men shouting on the hill below her. The shouts and the barking of dogs came nearer and nearer.

Then a dog ran up to her, and licked her face, and jumped about her.

It was her own sheepdog, *Yarrow*.

He ran back to the men who were following him, and came again with one of them.

It was old Simon Grieve, very tired, and so much out of breath that he could scarcely speak.

Jean was very glad to see him, and not frightened any longer.

"Oh, Jeanie, my doo'," said Simon, "where hae ye been? A muckle gliff ye hae gien us, and a weary spiel up the weary braes."

Jean told him all about it: how she had come with Randal to see the Wishing Well, and how she had lost him, and fallen asleep.

"And sic a nicht for you bairns to wander on the hill," said Simon. "It's the nicht o' St. John, when the guid folk hae power. And there's a' the lads burning the Bel fires, and driving the nowt* through them: nae less will serve them. Sic a nicht!"

* Nowt, cattle.

This was the cause of the fire Jean saw, and of the noise of the cattle. On midsummer's night the country people used to light these fires, and drive the cattle through them. It was an old, old custom come down from heathen times.

Now the other men from Fairnilee had gathered round Jean. Lady Ker had sent them out to look for Randal and her on the hills. They had heard from the good wife at Peel that the children had gone up the burn, and *Yarrow* had tracked them till Jean was found.

CHAPTER VII.

Where is Randal?

JEAN was found, but where was Randal? She told the men who had come out to look for her, that Randal had gone on to look for the Wishing Well. So they rolled her up in a big shepherd's plaid, and two of them carried Jean home in the plaid, while all the rest, with lighted torches in their hands, went to look for Randal through the wood.

Jean was so tired that she fell asleep again in her plaid before they reached Fairnilee. She was wakened by the men shouting as they drew near the house, to show that they were coming home. Lady Ker was waiting at the gate, and the old nurse ran down the grassy path to meet them.

"Where's my bairn?" she cried as soon as she was within call.

The men said, "Here's Mistress Jean, and Randal will be here soon; they have gone to look for him."

"Where are they looking?" cried nurse.

"Just about the Wishing Well."

The nurse gave a scream, and hobbled back to Lady Ker.

"Ma bairn's tint!"* she cried, "ma bairn's tint! They'll find him never. The good folk have stolen him away from that weary Wishing Well!"

"Hush, nurse," said Lady Ker, "do not frighten Jean."

She spoke to the men, who had no doubt that Randal would soon be found and brought home.

So Jean was put to bed, where she forgot all her troubles; and Lady Ker waited, waited, all night, till the grey light began to come in, about two in the morning.

Lady Ker kept very still and quiet, telling her beads, and praying. But the old nurse would never be still, but was always wandering out, down to the river's edge, listening for the shouts of the shepherds coming home. Then she would come back again, and moan and wring her hands, crying for "her bairn."

About six o'clock, when it was broad daylight and all the birds were singing, the men returned from the hill.

But Randal did not come with them.

Then the old nurse set up a great cry, as the country people do over the bed of someone who has just died.

Lady Ker sent her away, and called Simon Grieve to her own room.

"You have not found the boy yet?" she

* Tint, lost.

said, very stately and pale. "He must have wandered over into Yarrow; perhaps he has gone as far as Newark, and passed the night at the castle, or with the shepherd at Foulshiels."

"No, my Lady," said Simon Grieve, "some o' the men went over to Newark, and some to Foulshiels, and other some down to Sir John Murray's at Philiphaugh; but there's never a word o' Randal in a' the country-side."

"Did you find no trace of him?" said Lady Ker, sitting down suddenly in the great arm-chair.

"We went first through the wood, my Lady, by the path to the Wishing Well. And he had been there, for the whip he carried in his hand was lying on the grass. And we found *this*."

He put his hand in his pouch, and brought out a little silver crucifix, that Randal used always to wear round his neck on a chain.

"This was lying on the grass beside the Wishing Well, my Lady——"

Then he stopped, for Lady Ker had swooned away. She was worn out with watching and with anxiety about Randal.

Simon went and called the maids, and they brought water and wine, and soon Lady Ker came back to herself, with the little silver crucifix in her hand.

The old nurse was crying, and making a great noise.

"The good folk have taken ma bairn," she said, "this nicht o' a' the nichts in the year, when the fairy folk—preserve us frae them!—have power. But they could nae take the blessed rood o' grace; it was beyond their strength. If gipsies, or robber folk frae the Debatable Land, had carried away the bairn, they would hae taken him, cross and a'. But the guid folk have gotten him, and Randal Ker will never, never mair come hame to bonny Fairnilee."

What the old nurse said was what everybody thought. Even Simon Grieve shook his head, and did not like it.

But Lady Ker did not give up hope. She sent horsemen through all the country-side: up Tweed to the Crook, and to Talla; up Yarrow, past Catslack Tower, and on to the Loch of Saint Mary; up Ettrick to Thirlestane and Buccleugh, and over to Gala, and to Branxholme in Teviotdale; and even to Hermitage Castle, far away by Liddel water.

They rode far and rode fast, and at every cottage and every tower they asked "had any-one seen a boy in green?" But nobody had seen Randal through all the country-side. Only a shepherd lad, on Foulshiels hill, had heard bells ringing in the night, and a sound of laughter go past him, like a breeze of wind over the heather.

Days went by, and all the country was out

to look for Randal. Down in Yetholme they sought him, among the gipsies; and across the Eden in merry Carlisle; and through the Land Debatable, where the robber Armstrongs and Grahames lived; and far down Tweed, past Melrose, and up Jed water, far into the Cheviot hills.

But there never came any word of Randal. He had vanished as if the earth had opened and swallowed him. Father Francis came from Melrose Abbey, and prayed with Lady Ker, and gave her all the comfort he could. He shook his head when he heard of the Wishing Well, but he said that no spirit of earth or air could have power for ever over a Christian soul. But, even when he spoke, he remembered that, once in seven years, the fairy folk have to pay a dreadful tax, one of themselves, to the King of a terrible country of Darkness; and what if they had stolen Randal, to pay the tax with *him!*

This was what troubled good Father Francis, though, like a wise man, he said nothing about it, and even put the thought away out of his own mind.

But you may be sure that the old nurse had thought of this tax on the fairies too, and that *she* did not hold her peace about it, but spoke to everyone that would listen to her, and would have spoken to the mistress if she had been allowed. But when she tried to begin, Lady

Ker told her that she had put her own trust in Heaven, and in the Saints. And she gave the nurse such a look when she said that, "if ever Jean heard of this, she would send nurse away from Fairnilee, out of the country," that the old woman was afraid, and was quiet.

As for poor Jean, she was perhaps the most unhappy of them all. She thought to herself, if she had refused to go with Randal to the Wishing Well, and had run in and told Lady Ker, then Randal would never have started to find the Wishing Well. And she put herself in great danger, as she fancied, to find him. She wandered alone on the hills, seeking all the places that were believed to be haunted by fairies.

At every Fairy Knowe, as the country people called the little round green knolls in the midst of the heather, Jean would stoop her ear to the ground, trying to hear the voices of the fairies within. For it was believed that you might hear the sound of their speech, and the trampling of their horses, and the shouts of the fairy children. But no sound came, except the song of the burn flowing by, and the hum of gnats in the air, and the *gock, gock,* the cry of the grouse, when you frighten him in the heather.

Then Jeanie would try another way of meeting the fairies, and finding Randal. She would walk nine times round a Fairy Knowe, beginning from the left side, because then it was fancied that the hill-side would open, like a door, and show a path into Fairyland. But the hill-side never opened, and she never saw a single fairy; not even old Whuppity Stoorie sit with her spinning-wheel in a green glen, spinning grass into gold, and singing her fairy song:—

"I once was young and fair,
　　My eyes were bright and blue,
　　As if the sun shone through,
And golden was my hair.

"Down to my feet it rolled
　　Ruddy and ripe like corn,
　　Upon an autumn morn,
In heavy waves of gold.

"Now am I grey and old,
　　And so I sit and spin,
　　With trembling hand and thin,
This metal bright and cold.

"I would give all the gain,
　　These heaps of wealth untold
　　Of hard and glittering gold,
Could I be young again!"

CHAPTER VIII.

The Ill Years.

SO autumn came, and all the hill-sides were golden with the heather; and the red coral berries of the rowan trees hung from the boughs, and were wet with the spray of the waterfalls in the burns. And days grew shorter, and winter came with snow, but Randal never came back to Fairnilee. Season after season passed, and year after year. Lady Ker's hair grew white like snow, and her face thin and pale—for she fasted often, as was the rule of her Church; all this was before the Reformation. And she slept little, praying half the night for Randal's sake. And she went on pilgrimages to many shrines of the Saints: to St. Boswell and St. Rule's, hard by the great Cathedral of St. Andrew's on the sea. Nay, she went across the Border as far as the Abbey of St. Alban's, and even to St. Thomas's shrine of Canterbury, taking Jean with her. Many a weary mile they rode over hill and dale, and many an adventure they had, and ran many dangers from robbers, and soldiers disbanded from the wars.

But at last they had to come back to Fairnilee; and a sad place it was, and silent without the sound of Randal's voice in the hall, and the noise of his hunting-horn in the woods. None of the people wore mourning for him, though they mourned in their hearts. For to put on black would look as if they had given up all hope. Perhaps most of them thought they would never see him again, but Jeanie was not one who despaired.

The years that had turned Lady Ker's hair white, had made Jean a tall, slim lass—"very bonny," everyone said; and the country people called her the Flower of Tweed. The Yarrow folk had their Flower of Yarrow, and why not the folk of Tweedside? It was now six years since Randal had been lost, and Jeanie was grown a young woman, about seventeen years old. She had always kept a hope that if Randal was with the Fairy Queen he would return perhaps in the seventh year. People said on the country-side that many a man and woman had escaped out of Fairyland after seven years' imprisonment there.

Now the sixth year since Randal's disappearance began very badly, and got worse as it went on. Just when spring should have been beginning, in the end of February, there came the most dreadful snowstorm. It blew and snowed, and blew again, and the snow was as fine as the dust on a road in summer. The strongest shepherds could not hold their own against the tempest, and were "smoored" (or smothered) in the waste. The flocks moved down from the hill-sides, down and down, till all the sheep on a farm would be gathered together in a crowd, under the shelter of a wood in some deep dip of the hills. The storm seemed as if it would never cease; for thirteen days the snow drifted and the wind blew. There was nothing for the sheep to eat, and if there had been hay enough, it would have been impossible to carry it to them. The poor beasts bit at the wool on each other's backs, and so many of them died that the shepherds built walls with the dead bodies to keep the wind and snow away from those that were left alive.

There could be little work done on the farm that spring; and summer came in so cold and wet that the corn could not ripen, but was levelled to the ground. Then autumn was rainy, and the green sheaves lay out in the fields, and sprouted and rotted; so that little corn was reaped, and little flour could be made that year. Then in winter, and as spring came on, the people began to starve. They had no grain, and there were no potatoes in those days, and no rice; nor could corn be brought in from foreign countries. So men and women and children might be seen in the fields, with white pinched faces, gathering nettles to make soup, and digging for roots that were often little better than poison. They ground the bark of the fir trees, and mixed it with the little flour they could get; and they ate such beasts as never are eaten except in time of famine.

It is said that one very poor woman and her daughter always looked healthy and plump in these dreadful times, till people began to suspect them of being witches. And they were taken, and charged before the Sheriff with living by witchcraft, and very likely they would have been burned. So they confessed that they had fed ever since the famine began—on snails! But there were not snails enough for all the country-side, even if people had cared to eat them. So many men and women died, and more were very weak and ill.

Lady Ker spent all her money in buying food for her people. Jean and she lived on as little as they could, and were as careful as they could be. They sold all the beautiful silver plate, except the cup that Randal's father used to drink out of long ago. But almost everything else was sold to buy corn.

So the weary year went on, and Midsummer Night came round—the seventh since the night when Randal was lost.

Then Jean did what she had always meant to do. In the afternoon she slipped out of the house of Fairnilee, taking a little bread in a basket, and saying that she would go to see the farmer's wife at Peel, which was on the other side of Tweed. But her mind was to go to the Wishing Well. There she would wish for Randal back again, to help his mother in the evil times. And if she, too, passed away as he had passed out of sight and hearing, then at

least she might meet him in that land where he had been carried. How strange it seemed to Jean to be doing everything over again that she had done seven years before. Then she had been a little girl, and it had been hard work for her to climb up the side of the Peel burn. Now she walked lightly and quickly, for she was tall and well-grown. Soon she reached the crest of the first hill, and remembered how she had sat down there and cried, when she was a child, and how the flies had tormented her. They were buzzing and teasing still; for good times or bad make no difference to them, as long as the sun shines. Then she reached the cairn at the top of the next hill, and far below her lay the forest, and deep within it ran Yarrow, glittering like silver.

Jean paused a few moments, and then struck into a green path which led through the wood. The path wound beneath dark pines; their topmost branches were red in the evening light, but the shade was black beneath them. Soon the path reached a little grassy glade, and there among cold, wet grasses was the Wishing Well. It was almost hidden by the grass, and looked very black, and cool, and deep. A tiny trickle of water flowed out of it, flowed down to join the Yarrow. The trees about it had scraps of rags and other things pinned to them, offerings made by the country people to the spirits of the well.

CHAPTER IX.

The White Roses.

JEANIE sat down beside the well. She wished her three wishes: to see Randal, to win him back from Fairyland, and to help the people in the famine. Then she knelt on the grass, and looked down into the well-water. At first she saw nothing but the smooth black water, with little waves trembling in it. Then the water began to grow bright within, as if the sun was shining far, far below. Then it grew as clear as crystal, and she saw through it, like a glass, into a new country—a beautiful country with a wide green plain, and in the midst of the plain a great castle, with golden flags floating from the tops of all the towers. Then she heard a curious whispering noise that thrilled and murmured, as if the music of all the trees that the wind blows through the world were in her ears, as if the noise of all the waves of every sea, and the rustling of heather-bells on every hill, and the singing of all birds were sounding, low and sweet, far, far away. Then she saw a great company of knights and ladies, dressed in green, ride up to the castle; and one knight rode apart from the rest, on a milk-white steed. They all went into the castle gates; but this knight rode slowly and sadly behind the others, with his head bowed on his breast.

Then the musical sounds were still, and the castle and the plain seemed to wave in the water. Next they quite vanished, and the well grew dim, and then grew dark and black and smooth as it had been before. Still she looked, and the little well bubbled up with sparkling foam, and so became still again, like a mirror, till Jeanie could see her own face in it, and beside her face came the reflection of another face, a young man's, dark, and sad, and beautiful. The lips smiled at her, and then Jeanie knew it was Randal. She thought he must be looking over her shoulder, and she leaped up with a cry, and glanced round.

But she was all alone, and the wood about her was empty and silent. The light had gone out of the sky, which was pale like silver, and overhead she saw the evening star.

Then Jeanie thought all was over. She had seen Randal as if it had been in a glass, and she hardly knew him: he was so much older, and his face was so sad. She sighed, and turned to go away over the hills, back to Fairnilee.

But her feet did not seem to carry her the way she wanted to go. It seemed as if something within her were moving her in a kind of dream. She felt herself going on through the forest, she did not know where. Deeper into the wood she went, and now it grew so dark that she saw scarce anything; only she felt the fragrance of briar roses, and it seemed to her that she was guided towards these roses. Then she knew there was a hand in her hand, though she saw nobody, and the hand seemed to lead her on. And she came to an open place in the forest, and there the silver light fell clear from the sky, and she saw a great shadowy rose tree, covered with white wild roses.

The hand was still in her hand, and Jeanie began to wish for nothing so much in the world as to gather some of these roses. She put out her hand and she plucked one, and there before her stood a strange creature—a dwarf, dressed in yellow and red, with a very angry face.

"Who are you," he cried, "that pluck my roses without my will?"

"And who are *you?*" said Jeanie, trembling, "and what right have you on the hills of this world?"

Then she made the holy sign of the cross, and the face of the elf grew black, and the light went out of the sky.

She only saw the faint glimmer of the white flowers, and a kind of shadow standing where the dwarf stood.

"I bid you tell me," said Jeanie, "whether you are a Christian man, or a spirit that dreads the holy sign," and she crossed him again.

Now all grew dark as the darkest winter's night. The air was warm and deadly still, and heavy with the scent of the fairy flowers.

In the blackness and the silence, Jeanie made

the sacred sign for the third time. Then a clear fresh wind blew on her face, and the forest boughs were shaken, and the silver light grew and gained on the darkness, and she began to see a shape standing where the dwarf had stood. It was far taller than the dwarf, and the light grew and grew, and a star looked down out of the night, and Jean saw Randal standing by her. And she kissed him, and he kissed her, and he put his hand in hers, and they went out of the wood together. They came to the crest of the hill and the cairn. Far below them they saw the Tweed shining through an opening among the trees, and the lights in the farm of Peel, and they heard the nightbirds crying, and the bells of the sheep ringing musically as they wandered through the fragrant heather on the hills.

CHAPTER X.

Out of Fairyland.

YOU may fancy, if you can, what joy there was in Fairnilee when Randal came home. They quite forgot the hunger and the hard times, and the old nurse laughed and cried over her bairn that had grown into a tall, strong young man. And to Lady Ker it was all one as if her husband had come again, as he was when first she knew him long ago; for Randal had his face, and his eyes, and the very sound of his voice. They could hardly believe he was not a spirit, and they clasped his hands, and hung on his neck, and could not keep their eyes off him. This was the end of all their sorrow, and it was as if Randal had come back from the dead; so that no people in the world were ever so happy as they were next day, when the sun shone down on the Tweed and the green trees that rustle in the wind round Fairnilee. But in the evening, when the old nurse was out of the way, Randal sat between his mother and Jean, and they each held his hands, as if they could not let him go, for fear he should vanish away from them again. And they would turn round anxiously if anything stirred, for fear it should be the two white deer that sometimes were said to come for people escaped from Fairyland, and then these people must rise and follow them, and never return any

more. But the white deer never came for Randal.

So he told them all his adventures, and all that had happened to him since that midsummer night, seven long years ago.

It had been with him as it was with Jean. He had gone to the Wishing Well, and wished to see the Fairy Queen and Fairyland. And he had seen the beautiful castle in the well, and a beautiful woman's face had floated up

to meet his on the water. Then he had gathered the white roses, and then he heard a great sound of horses' feet, and of bells jingling, and a lady rode up, the very lady he had seen in the well. She had a white horse, and she was dressed in green, and she beckoned to Randal to mount on her horse, with her before him on the pillion. And the bells on the bridle rang, and the horse flew faster than the wind.

So they rode and rode through the summer night, and they came to a desert place, and living lands were left far behind. Then the Fairy Queen showed him three paths, one steep and narrow, and beset with briars and thorns: that was the road to goodness and happiness, but it was little trodden or marked with the feet of people that had come and gone.

And there was a wide smooth road that went through fields of lilies, and that was the path of easy living and pleasure.

The third path wound about the wild hill-side, through ferns and heather, and that was the way to Elfland, and that way they rode. And still they rode through a country of dark night, and they crossed great black rivers, and they saw neither sun nor moon, but they heard the roaring of the sea. From that country they came into the light, and into the beautiful garden that lies round the castle of the Fairy Queen. There they lived in a noble company of gallant knights and fair ladies. All seemed very mirthful, and they rode, and hunted, and danced; and it was never dark night, nor broad daylight, but like early summer dawn before the sun has risen.

There Randal said that he had quite forgotten his mother and Jean, and the world where he was born, and Fairnilee.

But one day he happened to see a beautiful golden bottle of a strange shape, all set with diamonds, and he opened it. There was in it a sweet-smelling water, as clear as crystal, and he poured it into his hand, and passed his hand over his eyes. Now this water had the power to destroy the "glamour" in Fairyland, and make people see it as it really was. And when Randal touched his eyes with it, lo, everything was changed in a moment. He saw that nothing was what it had seemed. The gold vanished from the embroidered curtains, the light grew dim and wretched like a misty winter day. The Fairy Queen, that had seemed so happy and beautiful in her bright dress, was a weary, pale woman in black, with a melancholy face and melancholy eyes. She looked as if she had been there for thousands of years,

always longing for the sunlight and the earth, and the wind and rain. There were sleepy poppies twisted in her hair, instead of a golden crown. And the knights and ladies were changed. They looked but half alive; and some, in place of their gay green robes, were dressed in rusty mail, pierced with spears and stained with blood. And some were in burial robes of white, and some in dresses torn or dripping with water, or marked with the burning of fire. All were dressed strangely in some ancient fashion; their weapons were old-fashioned, too, unlike any that Randal had ever seen on earth. And their festivals were not of dainty meats, but of cold, tasteless flesh, and of beans, and pulse, and such things as the old heathens, before the coming of the Gospel, used to offer to the dead. It was dreadful to see them at such feasts, and dancing, and riding, and pretending to be merry with hollow faces and unhappy eyes.

And Randal wearied of Fairyland, which now that he saw it clearly looked like a great unending stretch of sand and barren grassy country, beside a grey sea where there was no tide. All the woods were of black cypress trees and poplar, and a wind from the sea drove a sea-mist through them, white and cold, and it blew through the open courts of the fairy castle.

So Randal longed more and more for the

old earth he had left, and the changes of summer and autumn, and the streams of Tweed, and the hills, and his friends. Then the voice of Jeanie had come down to him, sounding from far away. And he was sent up by the Fairy Queen in a fairy form, as a hideous dwarf, to frighten her away from the white roses in the enchanted forest.

But her goodness and her courage had saved him, for he was a christened knight, and not a man of the fairy world. And he had taken his own form again beneath her hand, when she signed him with the Cross, and here he was, safe and happy, at home at Fairnilee.

CHAPTER XI.

The Fairy Bottle.

WE soon grow used to the greatest changes, and almost forget the things that we were accustomed to before. In a day or two, Randal had nearly forgotten what a dull life he had lived in Fairyland, after he had touched his eyes with the strange water in the fairy bottle. He remembered the long, grey sands, and the cold mist, and the white faces of the strange people, and the gloomy queen, no more than you remember the dream you dreamed a week ago. But he did notice that Fairnilee was not the happy place it had been before he went away. Here, too, the faces were pinched and white, and the people looked hungry. And he missed many things that he remembered: the silver cups, and plates, and tankards. And the dinners were not like what they had been, but only a little thin soup, and some oatmeal cakes, and trout taken from the Tweed. The beef and ale of old times were not to be found, even in the houses of the richer people.

Very soon Randal heard all about the famine;

you may be sure the old nurse was ready to tell him all the saddest stories.

> " Full many a place in evil case
> Where joy was wont afore, oh!
> Wi' Humes that dwell in Leader braes,
> And Scotts that dwell in Yarrow! "

And the old woman would croon her old prophecies, and tell them how Thomas the Rhymer, that lived in Ercildoune, had foretold all this. And she would wish they could find these hidden treasures that the rhymes were full of, and that maybe were lying—who knew?—quite near them on their own lands.

"Where is the Gold of Fairnilee?" she would cry; "and, oh, Randal! can you no dig for it, and find it, and buy corn out of England for the poor folk that are dying at your doors?

> ' Atween the wet ground and the dry
> The Gold o' Fairnilee doth lie.'

There it is, with the sun never glinting on it; there it may bide till the Judgment-day, and no man the better for it.

> ' Between the Camp o' Rink
> And Tweed water clear,
> Lie nine kings' ransoms
> For nine hundred year.' "

"I doubt it's fairy gold, nurse," said Randal, "and would all turn black when it saw the sun.

It would just be like this bottle, the only thing I brought with me out of Fairyland."

Then Randal put his hand in his velvet pouch, and brought out a curious small bottle.* It was shaped like this, and was made of something that none of them had ever seen before. It was black, and you could see the light through it, and there were green and yellow spots and streaks on it.

"That ugly bottle looked like gold and diamonds when I found it in Fairyland," said Randal, "and the water in it smelled as sweet as roses. But when I touched my eyes with it, a drop that ran into my mouth was as salt as the sea, and immediately everything changed: the gold bottle became this glass thing, and the fairies became like folk dead, and the sky grew grey, and all turned waste and ugly. That's the way with fairy gold, nurse; and if you found it, even, it would all be dry leaves and black bits of coal before the sun set."

"Maybe so, and maybe no," said the old nurse. "The Gold o' Fairnilee may no be fairy gold, but just wealth o' this world that folk buried here lang syne. But noo, Randal, ma bairn, I maun gang out and see ma sister's son's dochter, that's lying sair sick o' the kin-

* In bottles like this, the old Romans used to keep their tears for their dead friends.

cough* at Rink, and take her some of the physic that I gae you and Jean when you were bairns."

So the old nurse went out, and Randal and Jean began to be sorry for the child she was going to visit. For they remembered the taste of the physic that the old nurse made by boiling the bark of elder-tree branches; and I remember it too, for it was the very nastiest thing that ever was tasted, and did nobody any good after all.

Then Randal ánd Jean walked out, strolling along without much noticing where they went, and talking about the pleasant days when they were children.

* Kincough, whooping cough.

CHAPTER XII.

At the Catrail.

THEY had climbed up the slope of a hill, and they came to a broad old ditch, beneath the shade of a wood of pine trees. Below them was a wide marsh, all yellow with marsh flowers, and above them was a steep slope made of stones. Now the dry ditch, where they sat down on the grass, looking towards the Tweed, with their backs to the hill, was called the *Catrail*. It ran all through that country, and must have been made by men very long ago. Nobody knows who made it, nor why. They did not know in Randal's time, and they do not know now. They do not even know what the name *Catrail* means, but that is what it has always been called. The steep slope of stone above them was named the Camp of Rink; it is a round place, like a ring, and no doubt it was built by the old Britons, when they fought against the Romans, many hundreds of years ago. The stones of which it is built are so large that we cannot tell how men moved them. But it is a very pleasant, happy place on a warm summer day, like the day when Randal and Jean sat there, with the daisies at their feet, and the wild doves cooing above their heads, and the rabbits running in and out among the ferns.

Jean and Randal talked about this and that, chiefly of how some money could be got to buy corn and cattle for the people. Randal was in favour of crossing the Border at night, and driving away cattle from the English side, according to the usual custom.

"Every day I expect to see a pair of spurs in a dish for all our dinner," said Randal.

That was the sign the lady of the house in the Forest used to give her men, when all the beef was done, and more had to be got by fighting.

But Jeanie would not hear of Randal taking spear and jack, and putting himself in danger by fighting the English. They were her own people after all, though she could not remember them and the days before she was carried out of England by Simon Grieve.

"Then," said Randal, "am I to go back to Fairyland, and fetch more gold like this ugly thing?" and he felt in his pocket for the fairy bottle.

But it was not in his pocket.

"What have I done with my fairy treasure?" cried Randal, jumping up. Then he stood still quite suddenly, as if he saw something strange.

He touched Jean on the shoulder, making a sign to her not to speak.

Jean rose quietly, and looked where Randal pointed, and this was what she saw.

She looked over a corner of the old grassy ditch, just where the marsh and the yellow flowers came nearest to it.

Here there stood three tall grey stones, each about as high as a man. Between them, with her back to the single stone, and between the two others facing Randal and Jean, the old nurse was kneeling.

If she had looked up, she could hardly have seen Randal and Jean, for they were within the ditch, and only their eyes were on the level of the rampart.

Besides, she did not look up; she was groping in the breast of her dress for something, and her eyes were on the ground.

"What can the old woman be doing?" whispered Randal. "Why, she has got my fairy bottle in her hand!"

Then he remembered how he had shown her the bottle, and how she had gone out without giving it back to him.

Jean and he watched, and kept very quiet.

They saw the old nurse, still kneeling, take the stopper out of the black strange bottle, and turn the open mouth gently on her hand. Then she carefully put in the stopper, and rubbed her eyes with the palm of her hand. Then she crawled along in their direction, very slowly, as if she were looking for something in the grass.

Then she stopped, still looking very closely at the grass.

Next she jumped to her feet with a shrill cry, clapping her hands; and then she turned, and was actually *running* along the edge of the marsh, towards Fairnilee.

"Nurse!" shouted Randal, and she stopped suddenly, in a fright, and let the fairy bottle fall.

It struck on a stone, and broke to pieces with a jingling sound, and the few drops of strange water in it ran away into the grass.

"Oh, ma bairns, ma bairns, what have you made me do?" cried the old nurse pitifully. "The fairy gift is broken, and maybe the Gold of Fairnilee, that my eyes have looked on, will ne'er be seen again."

CHAPTER XIII.

The Gold of Fairnilee.

RANDAL and Jean went to the old woman and comforted her, though they could not understand what she meant. She cried and sobbed, and threw her arms about; but, by degrees, they found out all the story.

When Randal had told her how all he saw in Fairyland was changed after he had touched his eyes with the water from the bottle, the old woman remembered many tales that she had heard about some charm known to the fairies, which helped them to find things hidden, and to see through walls and stones. Then she had got the bottle from Randal, and had stolen out, meaning to touch her eyes with the water, and try whether *that* was the charm and whether she could find the treasure spoken of in the old rhymes. She went

"Between the Camp o' Rink
And Tweed water clear,"

and to the place which lay

"Between the wet land and the dry,"

that is, between the marsh and the Catrail.

Here she had noticed the three great stones, which made a kind of chamber on the hill-side, and here she had anointed her eyes with the salt water of the bottle of tears.

Then she had seen through the grass, she declared, and through the upper soil, and she had beheld great quantities of gold. And she was running with the bottle to tell Randal, and to touch his eyes with the water that he might see it also. But, out of Fairyland, the strange water only had its magical power while it was still wet on the eyelashes. This the old nurse soon found; for she went back to the three standing stones, and looked and saw nothing, only grass and daisies. And the fairy bottle was broken, and all the water spilt.

This was her story, and Randal did not know what to believe. But so many strange things had happened to him, that one more did not seem impossible. So he and Jean took the old nurse home, and made her comfortable in her room, and Jean put her to bed, and got her a little wine and an oat-cake.

Then Randal very quietly locked the door outside, and put the key in his pocket. It would have been of no use to tell the old nurse to be quiet about what she thought she had seen.

By this time it was late and growing dark. But that night there would be a moon.

After supper, of which there was very little, Lady Ker went to bed. But Randal and Jean slipped out into the moonlight. They took a sack with them, and Randal carried a pickaxe and a spade. They walked quickly to the three great stones, and waited for a while to hear if all was quiet. Then Jean threw a white cloak round her, and stole about the edges of the camp and the wood. She knew that if any wandering man came by, he would not stay long where such a figure was walking. The night was cool, the dew lay on the deep fern; there was a sweet smell from the grass and from the pine wood.

In the meantime, Randal was digging a long trench with his pickaxe, above the place where the old woman had knelt, as far as he could remember it.

He worked very hard, and when he was in the trench up to his knees, his pickaxe struck against a stone. He dug round it with the spade, and came to a layer of black burnt ashes of bones. Beneath these, which he scraped away, was the large flat stone on which his pick had struck. It was a wide slab of red sandstone, and Randal soon saw that it was the lid of a great stone coffin, such as the ploughshare sometimes strikes against when men are ploughing the fields in the Border country.

Randal had seen these before, when he was a boy, and he knew that there was never much in them, except ashes and one or two rough pots of burnt clay.

He was much disappointed.

It had seemed as if he was really coming to something, and, behold, it was only an old stone coffin!

However, he worked on till he had cleared the whole of the stone coffin-lid. It was a very large stone chest, and must have been made, Randal thought, for the body of a very big man.

With the point of his pickaxe he raised the lid.

In the moonlight he saw something of a strange shape.

He put down his hand, and pulled it out.

It was an image, in metal, about a foot high, and represented a beautiful woman, with wings on her shoulders, sitting on a wheel.

Randal had never seen an image like this; but in an old book, which belonged to the Monks of Melrose, he had seen, when he was a boy, a picture of such a woman.

The Monks had told him that she was Fortune, with her swift wings that carry her from one person to another, as luck changes, and with her wheel that she turns with the turning of chance in the world.

The image was very heavy. Randal rubbed some of the dirt and red clay off, and found that the metal was yellow. He cut it with his knife; it was soft. He cleaned a piece, which shone bright and unrusted in the moonlight, and touched it with his tongue. Then he had no doubt any more. *The image was gold!*

Randal knew now that the old nurse had not been mistaken. With the help of the fairy water she had seen THE GOLD OF FAIRNILEE. He called very softly to Jeanie, who came glimmering in her white robes through the wood, looking herself like a fairy. He put the

image in her hand, and set his finger on his lips to show that she must not speak.

Then he went back to the great stone coffin, and began to grope in it with his hands. There was much earth in it that had slowly sifted through during the many years that it had been buried. But there was also a great round bowl of metal and a square box.

Randal got out the bowl first. It was covered with a green rust, and had a lid; in short, it was a large ancient kettle, such as soldiers use in camp. Randal got the lid off, and, behold, it was all full of very ancient gold coins, not Greek, nor Roman, but like *this*, such as were used in Briton before Julius Cæsar came.

The square box was of iron, and was rusted red. On the lid, in the moonshine, Jeanie could read the letters S. P. Q. R., but she did not know what they meant. The box had been locked, and chained, and clamped with iron bars. But all was so rusty that the bars were easily broken, and the lid torn off.

Then the moon shone on bars of gold, and on great plates and dishes of gold and silver, marked with letters, and with what Randal thought were crests. Many of the cups were studded with red and green and blue stones. And there were beautiful plates and dishes, purple, gold, and green; and one of these fell, and broke into a thousand pieces, for it was of some strange kind of glass. There were three gold sword-hilts, carved wonderfully into the figures of strange beasts with wings, and heads like lions.

Randal and Jean looked at it and marvelled, and Jean sang in a low, sweet voice:

> "Between the Camp o' Rink
> And Tweed water clear,
> Lie nine kings' ransoms
> For nine hundred year."

Nobody ever saw so much treasure in all broad Scotland.

Jean and Randal passed the rest of the night in hiding what they had found. Part they hid in the secret chamber of Fairnilee, of which only Jean and Lady Ker and Randal knew the secret. The rest they stowed away in various places. Then Randal filled the earth into the trench, and cast wood on the place, and set fire to the wood, so that next day there was nothing there but ashes and charred earth.

You will not need to be told what Randal did, now that he had treasure in plenty. Some he sold in France, to the king, Henry II., and some in Rome, to the Pope; and with the money which they gave him he bought corn and cattle in England, enough to feed all his neighbours, and stock the farms, and sow the fields for next year. And Fairnilee became a very rich and fortunate house, for Randal married Jean, and soon their children were playing on the banks of the Tweed, and rolling

down the grassy slope to the river, to bathe on hot days. And the old nurse lived long and happy among her new bairns, and often she told them how it was *she* who really found the Gold of Fairnilee.

You may wonder what the gold was, and how it came there? Probably Father Francis, the good Melrose Monk, was right. He said that the iron box and the gold image of Fortune, and the kettle full of coins, had belonged to some regiment of the Roman army: the kettle and the coins, they must have taken from the Britons; the box and all the plate were their own, and brought from Italy. Then they, in their turn, must have been defeated by some of the fierce tribes beyond the Roman wall, and must have lost all their treasure. That must have been buried by the victorious enemy; and *they*, again, must have been driven from their strong camp at Rink, either by some foes from the north, or by a new Roman army from the south. So all the gold lay at Fairnilee for many hundred years, never quite forgotten, as the old rhyme showed, but never found till it was discovered, in their sore need, by the old nurse and Randal and Jean.

As for Randal and Jean, they lived to be old, and died on one day, and they are buried at Dryburgh in one tomb, and a green tree grows over them; and the Tweed goes murmuring past their grave, and past the grave of Sir Walter Scott.

THE END.

PRINTING OFFICE OF THE PUBLISHER.

THE YELLOW FAIRY BOOK.

Edited by ANDREW LANG. With 22 Plates and 82 Illustrations in the Text by H. J. FORD. 12mo, cloth extra, gilt edges, $2.00.

CONTENTS:—The Cat and the Mouse in Partnership—The Six Swans—The Dragon of the North—Story of the Emperor's New Clothes—The Golden Crab—The Iron Stove—The Dragon and his Grandmother—The Donkey Cabbage—The Little Green Frog—The Seven-headed Serpent—The Grateful Beasts—The Giants and the Herd-boy—The Invisible Prince—The Crow—How Six Men Traveled Through the Wide World—The Wizard King—The Nixy—The Glass Mountain—Alphege ; or, The Green Monkey—Fairer-than-a-Fairy—The Three Brothers—The Boy and the Wolves; or, The Broken Promise—The Glass Axe—The Dead Wife—In the Land of Souls—The White Duck—The Witch and the Servants—The Magic Ring—The Flower Queen's Daughter—The Flying Ship—The Snow-daughter and the Fire-son—The Story of King Frost—The Death of the Sun-hero—The Witch—The Hazlenut Child—The Story of Big Klaus and Little Klaus—Prince Ring—The Swineherd—How to Tell a True Princess—The Blue Mountains—The Tinder-box—The Witch in the Stone-boat—Thumbelina—The Nightingale—Hermod and Hadvor—The Steadfast Tin-soldier—Blockhead Hans—A Story About a Darning-needle.

"'The Yellow Fairy Book' immediately takes place among the leading juvenile publications. . . . Mr. Lang's graceful and prepossessing style presents these old and yet ever new tales in charming text, and the numerous full-page and smaller illustrations by H. J. Ford are spirited and in complete harmony with the stories. . . . Without, it is one of the handsomest and within one of the most entertaining books the season can produce."—*Times*, Boston.

"Mr. Lang has a positive genius for knowing what will delight his youthful readers in this sort of literature and his mastery of folklore gives him a great advantage in the selection of material for his agreeable compilations. . . . He is careful not to include anything that can be offensive to good taste or good morals, and he has got together in this as in former collections, stories that deserve to be reckoned among the classics. . . . The imaginative element is strong, as it ought to be, and they have been most felicitously illustrated by H. J. Ford, who has a marvelous faculty for depicting strange monsters, witch-maidens, lovely princesses and fearless knights and making them appear like real creatures. Every healthy child should read fairy tales and cultivate his imagination, which in these days of scientific education is in danger of total extinction."—*Beacon*, Boston.

"It is rich with marvelous tales, adapted in Mr. Lang's charming style from Russian, German, French, Icelandic, and Red Indian folklore, stories that have their birth in the earliest imaginings of the human race, before knowledge obtained its destructive sway."—*Journal*, Chicago.

"As delightful and fascinating as any of its predecessors. . . . And the pictures—plenty of them, by H. J. Ford—are very charming and appropriate. The beautifully designed cover is just the thing for such a book. The boy or girl who owns a copy is indeed fortunate."—*Churchman*, New York.

"Not less fascinating than its predecessors. . . . The stories are charmingly told and equally charmingly illustrated by Mr. H. J. Ford. 'Joan, Toddles and Tiny,' to whom the book is dedicated, and their countless brothers and sisters, will find a rare treat in having these tales read to them."—*Outlook*, New York.

New York: Longmans, Green, & Co.

THE BLUE FAIRY BOOK.

Edited by ANDREW LANG. With 8 plates and 130 Illustrations in the Text. Crown 8vo, cloth, gilt, $2.00.

CONTENTS:—The Bronze Ring—Prince Hyacinth and the Dear Little Princess—East of the Sun and West of the Moon—The Yellow Dwarf—Little Red Riding Hood—The Sleeping Beauty in the Wood—Cinderella; or, The Little Glass Slipper—Aladdin and the Wonderful Lamp—The Tale of a Youth who Set Out to Learn What Fear Was—Rumpelstiltzkin—Beauty and the Beast—The Master Maid—Why the Sea is Salt—The Master Cat; or, Puss in Boots—Felicia and the Pot of Pinks—The White Cat—The Water-lily—The Goldspinners—The Terrible Head—The Story of Pretty Goldilocks—The History of Whittington—The Wonderful Sheep—Little Thumb—The Forty Thieves—Hansel and Grettel—Snow-white and Rose-red—The Goose-girl—Toads and Diamonds—Prince Darling—Blue Beard—Trusty John—The Brave Little Tailor—A Voyage to Lilliput—The Princess on the Glass Hill—The Story of Prince Ahmed and the Fairy Paribanou—The History of Jack the Giant Killer—The Black Bull of Norroway—The Red Etin.

"There could hardly be a better collection of fairy stories. Mr. Lang has picked from every source, rewritten, condensed, and adapted them until each is perfect in itself, and altogether form a model story book."—*Christian Union.*

"The loveliest collection of fairy stories that any Christmas holiday ever brought, and, with its exquisite charm of the stories rendered still more attractive by the pretty blue and gold fancy in binding. It is a part of the library of information to have these tales; both for children and grown people, they are a wonderful fountain for suggestion and allusion. They hold within themselves the poetry of the race. This exquisite collection will easily be treasured as a classic of English literature."—*Boston Traveller.*

"A well-chosen selection of the good old stories which have pleased many generations of young readers and will please many more."—*Independent.*

THE RED FAIRY BOOK.

Edited by ANDREW LANG. With 4 plates and 96 Illustrations in the Text. Crown 8vo, cloth, gilt, $2.00.

CONTENTS:—The Twelve Dancing Princesses—The Princess Mayblossom—Soria Moria Castle—The Death of Koschei the Deathless—The Black Thief and Knight of the Glen—The Master Thief—Brother and Sister—Princess Rosette—The Enchanted Pig—The Norka—The Wonderful Birch—Jack and the Beanstalk—The Good Little Mouse—Graciosa and Percinet—The Three Princesses of Whiteland—The Voice of Death—The Six Sillies—Kari Woodengown—Drakestail—The Ratcatcher—The True History of Little Goldenhood—The Golden Branch—The Three Dwarfs—Dapplegrim—The Enchanted Canary—The Twelve Brothers—Rapunzel—The Nettle Spinner—Farmer Weatherbeard—Mother Holle—Minnikin—Bushy Bride—Snowdrop—The Golden Goose—The Seven Foals—The Marvelous Musician—The Story of Sigurd.

"A delightful pendant to its Blue predecessor of last year. . . . Many of these tales will be found unfamiliar to the rank and file of American readers of fairy tales, and all are treated with taste and skill."—*Book Buyer.*

"There are many of them unfamiliar which enhances the value of the book immensely, for it consequently abounds in new delights for the lover of the quaint and fantastic tales. . . . For a gift book for children 'The Red Fairy Book' can be commended in the most unreserved terms."—*Times,* Boston.

New York: Longmans, Green, & Co.

THE GREEN FAIRY BOOK.

Edited by ANDREW LANG. With 13 Plates and 88 Illustrations in the Text. Crown 8vo, cloth, gilt, $2.00.

CONTENTS:—The Blue Bird—The Half-Chick—The Story of Caliph Stork—The Enchanted Watch—Rosanella—Sylvain and Jocosa—Fairy Gifts—Prince Narcissus and the Princess Potentilla—Prince Fatherhead and the Princess Celandine—The Three Little Pigs—Heart of Ice—The Enchanted Ring—The Snuff-box—The Golden Blackbird—The Magic Swan—The Dirty Shepherdess—The Enchanted Snake—The Biter Bit—King Kojata—Prince Fickle and Fair Helena—Puddocky—The Story of Hok Lee and the Dwarfs—The Story of the Three Bears—Prince Vivien and the Princess Placida—Little One-eye, Little Two-eyes, and Little Three-eyes—Jorinde and Joringel—Allerleirauh ; or, the Many-furred Creature—The Twelve Huntsmen—Spindle, Shuttle, and Needle—The Crystal Coffin—The Three Snake-leaves—The Riddle—Jack my Hedgehog—The Golden Lads—The White Snake—The Story of a Clever Tailor—The Golden Mermaid—The War of the Wolf and the Fox—The Story of the Fisherman and His Wife—The Three Musicians—The Three Dogs.

"Any child with a spark of imagination would revel in these charmed pages, where right makes might and courage is invariably rewarded. The many illustrations by Mr. H. J. Ford are an additional attraction."—*Dial*, Chicago.

"Mr. Lang . . . . shows himself here to be in thorough sympathy with the tastes and tenderness of children, and the result of his editorial tact and care is a most delightful book. Happy will be the boy or girl who comes into possession of this beautiful volume at the coming Christmas season."
—*Christian at Work*, N. Y.

THE BLUE POETRY BOOK.

Edited by ANDREW LANG. With 12 Plates and 88 Illustrations in the Text. Crown 8vo, cloth, gilt, $2.00.

The purpose of this collection is to put before children, and young people, poems which are good in themselves, and especially fitted to live, as Theocritus says, on the lips of the young. The editor has been guided to a great extent, in making his choice, by recollections of what particularly pleased himself in youth.
—EXTRACT FROM PREFACE.

"Is a pleasing and satisfactory completion of poetry, most of which is known and held in high estimation by all persons of taste and education. The selection is most judicious, and the most carping critic would be hard set to raise an objection. . . . The selection is not confined to poems for the young, but includes many of the noblest poems in the English language which not to know is to confess ourselves imperfectly educated."—*Commercial Advertiser*.

"The collection is excellently chosen, the pictures strikingly good, and the book a treasury of strong and fine verse. The contents are best summarized by assuring you that any poem which ought to be there is there ; and none that are included should have been left out. It is an exquisite book, representing Mr. Lang's passion for the heroic, romantic and comic in verse, and having through its illustrations a fairy-like appearance that will catch the fancy of young readers."
—*The Book Buyer*.

New York: Longmans, Green, & Co.

THE TRUE STORY BOOK.

Edited by ANDREW LANG. With 9 Plates and 58 Illustrations in the Text. Crown 8vo, cloth, gilt, $2.00.

CONTENTS:—A Boy Among the Red Indians—Casanova's Escape—Adventures on the Findhorn—The Story of Grace Darling—The "Shannon" and the "Chesapeake"—Captain Snelgrave and the Pirates—The Spartan Three Hundred—Prince Charlie's Wanderings—Two Great Matches—The Story of Kaspar Hauser—An Artist's Adventure—The Tale of Isandhlwana and Rorke's Drift—How Leif the Lucky Found Vineland the Good—The Escape of Cervantes—The Worthy Enterprise of John Foxe—Baron Trenck—The Adventure of John Rawlins—The Chevalier Johnstone's Escape from Culloden—The Adventures of Lord Pitsligo—The Escape of Cæsar Borgia from the Castle of Medina del Campo—The Kidnapping of the Princes—The Conquest of Montezuma's Empire—The Return of the French Freebooters.

"The editor acknowledges that there is not a dragon in the whole collection, and that giants and witches are conspicuous by their absence, but there are princes, and marvelous escapes, and good fighting, and buccaneering, and the punishment of wicked conspirators to read about, so that the volume is not by any means lacking in heroic and romantic interest. . . . Parents may safely buy this book for their children with the assurance that it will cultivate their imaginative faculties in a healthful way and give them a vast amount of harmless pleasure."
—*Boston Beacon.*

"Striking adventure, fanciful plays of imagination that in no way disturb veracity, and the romance of truthful history are strung together in a way that will make the readers, young and old, realize that truth is stranger than fiction and makes wondrously entertaining reading."—*N. Y. Observer.*

"The author . . . has been extremely fortunate in the selection of subjects which will be eagerly read and will prove highly entertaining and instructive. It is in no sense a collection of fairy tales but a volume rich in adventures which actually happened to real people. . . . It is an admirable gift book for children."
—*Public Opinion,* N. Y.

THE OUTDOOR WORLD;
OR, THE YOUNG COLLECTOR'S HANDBOOK.

By W. FURNEAUX, F.R.G.S. With 546 Illustrations, including 16 colored Plates. Crown 8vo, 438 pages, ornamental cover, gilt edges, $2.50.

CONTENTS:—Part I. ANIMAL LIFE—Chap. I. Ponds and Streams. II. Insects and Insect Hunting. III. The Sea-shore. IV. Snails and Slugs. V. Spiders, Centipedes and Millepedes. VI. Reptiles and Reptile Hunting. VII. British Birds. VIII. British Mammals. Part II. THE VEGETABLE WORLD.—IX. Seaweeds. X. Fungi. XI. Mosses. XII. Ferns. XIII. Wild Flowers. XIV. Grasses. XV. Our Forest Trees. Part III. THE MINERAL WORLD.—XVI. Minerals and Fossils.

New York: Longmans, Green, & Co.

www.ingramcontent.com/pod-product-compliance
Lightning Source LLC
Chambersburg PA
CBHW030741230426

43667CB00007B/801